"Solely through Stu's tutelage grit and dogged persistence required to develop and hone my skills in the art of salesmanship. I attribute 100 percent of my success in the industry to this man's unwavering faith, knowledge, and support. I am blessed to know that I can always reach out and be pointed in the right direction whenever I need counsel. *A Win a Day* offers a candid look into the insightful mind of a seasoned professional who has spent his time in the trenches, emerging on the other side a veteran and giant of the industry. This book will appeal to anyone considering a future in sales or mid-career professionals looking for clarity about handling tough situations, finding inspiration, and achieving personal growth."

—**Christopher Smith**, Certified Pedorthist, Hanger Clinics

"Whether you're a new sales professional looking to build your career with a foundation of strong habits or a veteran salesperson with a desire to straighten out or sharpen your game, *A Win A Day* is a must-read. The insights offered in this book are proven strategies refined by the author's distinguished career in athletics, sales, and leadership development.

—**Tim Malloy**, author of *One Thing: Focus on Sales Leadership: Insight from top business executives on what it takes to be a great leader.*

"An exceptional work, well told by a writer who deftly blends the excitement of sports with the insights of self-help. Stu Wittner reveals a new way to think about achieving excellence in sports, business, and life. A true inspiration."

—**Mike Drake**, author of *Through Their Eyes: An Empathetic Sales Professional's Guide to Success*

"I was fortunate to work for Stu as a sales rep at Rockport. The principals, practices, and motivational tools in *A Win A Day* truly work. These tools were invaluable to me in my career as a sales rep, regional sales manager, and as a national sales manager in the shoe industry. No matter what industry you're in, follow these principals and you too will have "A Win A Day" in your career and in life.

—**Frank Annunziata,** Former Senior Vice President of Sales,
Cole Haan Shoe Company

"I'm extremely grateful to Stu Wittner for providing me a roadmap for how to effectively transition from a high school history teacher and coach (baseball and basketball) to a thriving sales professional. His master coaching and mentoring skills quickly got me up to speed and allowed me to be Regional Sales Winner in my second year and the National Salesman of the Year in my third at Converse. I owe so much of my sales and sales management success to him! Because of his skilled guidance and support along the way, Stu encouraged me to spread my wings and grow every season. His coaching lessons were always part of my daily/seasonal sales plan. I am highly motivated, yet Stu always found creative ways to push me to reach an even higher level!

If you desire to become a successful sales professional this book is a MUST READ!"

—**Bill Adams**, Former Senior Vice President
of North America Sales, New Era Cap Company

"When I read *A Win A Day*, I immediately went to my desk and wrote those words on a sticky note and put it on the wall next to my computer. Stu Wittner is an inspiring sales leader, and I couldn't be more appreciative to have learned from him. This book has me thinking, *What more can I do, what more can I give?* I know I will continue to look for my "Win a Day" in work and life."

—**Tracy Harris,** Territory Manager, Orthofeet

"Wow!!! *A Win A Day* written by my good friend Stu Wittner is an excellent read that I fully endorse. The words jump off the page like a college education for what it takes to be successful in the selling industry. Veterans of the profession will appreciate the notes, layups, and drills from this lifetime basketball player and coach, while those new to the field will grasp on to the real strategies about how to reach goals and the infield execution of how to get it done. *A Win a Day* puts you on the path to win for a lifetime."

—**Herm Sorcher,** President/Partner
Danbury Hat Tricks/Danbury Ice Arena

"*A Win A Day* is a must read! Having never been on the sales side of my career, Stu's leadership inspired me to become one of the top salespeople within my first year. This book exemplifies all the aspects of why and how to have a successful sales career and get A Win A Day!"

—**Betha Ertzberger,** Certified Pedorthist

# A WIN
# A DAY

# A WIN A DAY

## WHAT I LEARNED FROM BASKETBALL THAT MADE ME A SALES PROFESSIONAL

## STU WITTNER

Stonebrook Publishing
Saint Louis, Missouri

A STONEBROOK PUBLISHING BOOK
©2023, Stuart Wittner
This book was guided in development and
edited by Nancy L. Erickson, The Book Professor®
TheBookProfessor.com

All rights reserved. Published in the United States
by Stonebrook Publishing, a division of Stonebrook Enterprises, LLC,
Saint Louis, Missouri. No part of this book may be reproduced, scanned,
or distributed in any printed or electronic form without
written permission from the author.

Please do not participate in or encourage piracy of copyrighted materials
in violation of the author's rights.

Library of Congress Control Number: 2023913140

ISBN: 978-1-955711-28-9

www.stonebrookpublishing.net

PRINTED IN THE UNITED STATES OF AMERICA

This book is dedicated to my parents, my wife,
my in-laws, my children and their spouses,
our grandchildren,
and all my mentors and friends.
All have given me the love and support
to pursue my dreams.

As Neil Diamond wrote, "Did you ever read about a frog
who dreamed of being a king and then became one? Well,
except for the names and a few other changes, if you talk
about me, the story's the same one."

I feel like that, too.

# CONTENTS

# 1

# MY SLIDE INTO SALES

couldn't breathe. I was nauseous and in a cold sweat, sitting in an empty gym and staring at the day's practice schedule. I realized that the dream job I'd always wanted and was so fortunate to attain was something that I no longer wanted to do. I was scared. I thought I'd coach forever. What would I do with the rest of my life? What skills did I have? The only jobs I'd pursued were in coaching. No, I didn't seek a career in sales. The profession found me, and I'm so grateful it did.

Why do many companies search far and wide to hire athletes for sales positions? It's because every sport has a scoreboard, and sales professionals are measured and evaluated every day. To be successful in athletics and selling requires commitment, preparation, performance, review, and correction.

I've had three exciting, challenging, and rewarding careers. First as a basketball coach, starting at Clarke Central High School in Athens, Georgia, then at the University of Georgia, and then at Pace University in New York. My second career was having traditional sales and marketing positions as a rep and sales manager at Converse, Rockport, and Timberland.

My third career was an entrepreneurial phase working on start-up concepts in the medical device industry. In all three, selling was a critical skill.

As technology emerged in the 1980s, Dick Loynd, Chairman of Converse, said at a meeting, "No matter how much technology or any other new system that gets invented comes about, some SOB is still going to have to sell whatever it is to someone." He was right. It's always challenging to be prepared and organized and successfully secure that order.

We've all heard the phrase "low-hanging fruit." Only those who've never sold use that expression, usually some marketing folks or senior executives who've forgotten what it's like to be out there in front of customers. A professional sales rep knows that there are no easy, automatic sales. Every sale is hard to come by. Like coaching, every win should be celebrated because none come easy. I still fail often, occasionally walk out of meetings, or hang up the phone and ask myself, *How could I have been a better listener, asked a better follow-up question, or done more homework?*

**Every sale is hard to come by. Just like coaching a game, every win should be celebrated because none come easy.**

When you get that big order, the high feels like hitting the winning jump shot. It's a shot of adrenaline and accomplishment after a lot of work. Conversely, it can be disappointing when the buyer passes or waters down an order that could significantly contribute to their business.

In coaching, we always ask, "Are the highs from winning stronger than the lows from losing?" Most everyone in athletics agrees that the lows from losing are much stronger. You ask yourself, *What went wrong? What could have been done better?*

There's a statistic sheet that all coaches look at during half-time and after the game. When you've won the game, it's a quick glance. After a loss, you devour it. You study it while trying to eat a post-game dinner. You may have lost by three points and shot eleven for twenty from the foul line. Just four more shots could have made the difference.

Sometimes you get a decent order in selling, but it doesn't include a couple of new products that would have made the order larger and helped the account add new customers. Staring at the order form is like looking at that post-game stat sheet.

When I was twenty-three, I was named the head basketball coach at Pace University, a Division II college in New York City. I thought I would coach my whole life there. As it turned out, those few years were a small percentage of all the time I'd spend working. I learned many skills and lessons from playing and coaching that apply to selling, which is why sports is a key theme of this book.

Let's begin here. Addiction is a powerful word, and most times, it's related to harmful individual struggles. However, some obsessions are positive and inspire us to keep striving for the use of or participation in an activity. My addiction started at twelve years old. I was riding the elevator up to the fifth floor of a Jewish Center in Flatbush Brooklyn, and as the elevator opened, the sounds of basketballs being dribbled and sneakers squeaking on the gym's hardwood floor assaulted me. The unmistakable smell of lacquer wafted into my nose, and I had that first-day-of-school stomachache feeling. I could hear players calling out to each other, and I felt my heart racing.

Over the next several decades, I'd enter many gyms. They all had that same strong smell, not only of the lacquer but also the smell of sweat and the sounds of grunts and bodies banging into each other. I was nervous and on edge that day because I was there for the first time to try out for a basketball team. I wasn't sure I was good enough, and I didn't know anyone except a coach who'd approached me at a local park and asked if I'd be interested in playing on a team. I would spend countless hours in this gym and many others for the next several years.

The outdoor parks in Brooklyn didn't have nets on the goals. Someone said that the nets would be stolen if they hung them. I wondered how someone could get to the top of the basketball goal to remove the nets. Could that really be a problem? When I shot baskets at the park, I heard the metallic scrape of the basketball touching the metal hooks where the net should have been tied. Other times, there was no sound when the shot landed perfectly through the middle of the goal. If I'd made that shot in a gym, I would have heard the wonderful, soft swoosh of the ball passing through the nylon. That intoxicating sound became part of my addiction, as did many other aspects of coming under the influence and love of basketball.

What were some of the feelings and experiences that drew me to this game? There were physical challenges to learn, improving the required skills, and the exhaustion that came with a drenched T-shirt. No matter what I did, I couldn't stop sweating, which was intoxicating. To this day, I wear multiple shirts and a sweatshirt, and I measure my workout by how wet these shirts get.

There was the adrenaline and nervous energy before a game and the release of that energy as I ran up and down the court during the first few minutes. There was the cheering of the crowd and its reverberating sounds against the gym walls—so loud I couldn't hear my teammates calling to me or the coach yelling instructions during a timeout. I couldn't even hear the ball I was dribbling hit the floor. I could only feel it leaving and returning to my hand. It's like the quiet when you're underwater. There's an odd calm when you can't hear anything because it's so loud.

There's also the brotherhood and camaraderie with teammates that becomes a bond that lasts a lifetime. Many of my teammates attended our coach's funeral, and I hosted a reunion at my home. There were no handshakes, just strong hugs all around. We all felt as close as we did fifty years ago.

Basketball became the singular focus of my life. All I wanted to do was play the game and become as good a player as possible, and I always knew I wanted to coach. I wanted to call out the plays, instruct, teach, and be in the middle of time-out huddles. I wanted to draw up the plays the team would execute as they returned to the court.

I spent many hours at a park near our apartment in my youth and played with buddies and strangers. I practiced by myself if no one was around. I would shoot alone for hours and work on my game. I remember this one older fellow who also came to the park. We'd play one-on-one full-court games to one hundred points. At the end of each day, I'd take a hundred foul shots. My goal was to make ninety, and I then had to make ten in a row before I would leave. I still do that today—the ten in a row, not the hundred.

On weekends and holidays, I'd get to the park early in the morning and play all day. After a few games, we'd go to a corner candy store. I always had a sixteen-ounce Nedicks orange soda and two pretzels; on many days, that would be three or four sodas and six or eight pretzels, which was my daily diet. I guess that's why I often had double-digit cavities when I went to the dentist.

I learned many lessons playing all those hours, first playing against competitors my age, then going against much older kids, and then adults. I studied the nuances of team play and realized other players appreciated unselfish play. Everyone wants to shoot the ball, and what I enjoyed most was setting up other players for their shots. One of the best feelings on the court was when I would draw the defender to me and make a pass to a teammate so he could score.

Not all experiences were positive. I was rail thin, and stronger and older opponents often pounded my body. There was also the experience of being soundly defeated by much better players. As I improved, there were times when I was the much better player and remembered how it felt to be beaten badly, and I'd ease up a bit and not take advantage of the weaker player.

My heart rate always jumped when I heard the familiar sounds of a gym or an arena. I played in small gyms throughout New York City and then in high school and college facilities. In addition to hearing the bouncing balls and players calling out to each other, there was always that familiar lacquer smell.

My dad worked long hours as a New York City cab driver. My mom was a secretary at a community college. Their work ethic and conduct were stellar; I never wanted to disappoint them. Mom always worked; therefore, I was a latchkey kid. This refers to kids who came home from school and let themselves in because their parents were working. In our case, it was an apartment in Brooklyn. This early independence and responsibility greatly impacted my development as a young person and adult. Being on my own and responsible for taking care of myself at a young age made me realize that I was responsible for taking care of what I needed.

I had many night games and practices. When I was thirteen, I played on two travel teams. My routine was to come home from school, do my homework, and make myself dinner in the late afternoon. I was a terrible eater, and I cooked a steak and French fries almost every night.

When I was a junior in high school, I played in Harlem in games that would start at 10:00 p.m., midnight, or later. I took the train to 125th Street in Harlem. At sixteen, I was usually the only white person in the gym, playing against men. The play was rough and super physical. Those games were a turning point in my career. They toughened me up physically and mentally. I was so thankful that my parents allowed me to go into some rough places and pursue my dream of improving.

I also played on my high school basketball team at Erasmus Hall in Brooklyn, founded in 1787. There were six thousand students. My brother had gone there and told me how good the team was. My goal was to play on that team. As a senior, we won the borough of Brooklyn and played in the Final Four of New York City at Madison Square Garden. Several years later, I was fortunate to coach a few games at "the world's most famous arena."

As a freshman in college, I played at Pace University. I had a good season and was First Team All-Conference; however, I wanted to experience being away from the New York area and transferred to the University of Georgia. As a senior, I was an assistant coach at Clarke Central High School. I was offered a graduate assistant coach position at Georgia the following year. After one season, I moved on to Pace University as the assistant coach, and after one season, I became the head coach. I was the country's youngest full-time head college basketball coach at the time. I was twenty-three.

If anyone had told me when I was named the head coach at Pace University that I'd spend most of the next forty years working outside of basketball, I never would have believed them. I'd planned to coach my whole life. You never know what opportunities may come your way, so it's important to be open minded when different ones are presented.

I was a pretty good player and came under the guidance of several experienced and dedicated coaches. I learned how to teach the skills of the games, prepare a team, handle the many different personalities, and evaluate and recruit players. I observed what the life of a coach could be, and I wanted that life. There's a special bond between players and their coaches. John Wooden said, "A good coach can change a game. A great coach can change a life." I wanted to have those special connected feelings with the players I coached.

While many have said basketball is a simple game at its core, many moving parts are required to succeed. I grew up watching the New York Knicks of the 1970s, often referred to as one of the most intelligent teams ever to play. They were noted for their unselfish and team-oriented play. Watching them as a young player, they reinforced all the team principles of sharing the ball that the coaches I played for also emphasized.

**There's a special bond between players and their coaches. John Wooden said, "A good coach can change a game. A great coach can change a life."**

My dad loved sports but didn't know the game of basketball. We'd sit together and watch the Knicks' games, and I'd point out the fundamental and team concepts and the individual nuances in front of us on the screen. In essence, I was coaching and teaching my dad the basics of the game. Those times with my dad are some of my most cherished memories of being with him.

Most people who get into coaching do so on a part-time basis. I was fortunate that I was always full time and could spend all my time and energy coaching. There's so much to prepare a team for at the start of a season. The preparation includes a long list of team concepts, both offensively and defensively, and an enormous number of game situations. There's also a lot of individual skill work for each player, not to mention the team chemistry and individually monitoring each player's athletic, educational, and personal development. I often worried about how much we had to teach, how much the players understood, and how they'd perform.

As a player, I was always nervous on game day, but once the game started and I ran up and down the court a few times to get all that built-up energy out, I felt good. In coaching, it's a whole different feeling of angst and nervous energy—not only during the game but also all day. A coach must be aware of and make decisions regarding the individual players, how the team is executing, what the other team is doing, and how the referees call the game—and it's all happening simultaneously. Coaching involves multi-tasking at a supersonic pace. I had to be 100 percent focused on everything going on because if I missed the slightest change, it could affect the outcome. Paying attention to every detail during a game is critical, just like in a sales situation. Reading the buyer's reaction is similar to watching the players on the court.

As a young coach, I enjoyed practices more than games. One big reason was that every team we played against had a coach who was more experienced than me. I was learning on the job, but these men knew the job. I used to say that the other team's coach had the formula, and I was trying to learn the formula. That's an intimidating feeling. There is no substitute for experience in any field, whether athletics or business. As a rep, I had this same uncomfortable sensation that the buyer knew more than I did about the business, and this motivated me to prepare as best I could to learn as much as possible about my product and each customer.

**Paying attention to every detail during a game is critical, just like in a sales situation. Reading the buyer's reaction is similar to watching the players on the court.**

Since I'd played basketball myself, I had a good idea about how to run a university basketball program, but I still had a lot to learn. There are differences between being a player and an assistant coach—and even further differences between assistant coaches and head coaches. Assistants make suggestions; head coaches make decisions. Head coaches have a long list of responsibilities, including recruiting, planning, scheduling practices and games, and working with players. We also have administrative tasks such as working with admissions, financial aid, housing, transportation, and food services, to name a few. The job is not to just roll out the balls for practice. There's a lot more work to do.

I made a lot of mistakes as a young coach. I recruited the wrong players for the system I wanted to run in several cases, partly because recruiting players to a Division II school is difficult. I wound up settling for players I thought we could improve. While we developed the skills of all the players, in several cases, the players simply couldn't grasp the mental aspects of the game I taught.

One example was a junior college player from Florida we'd recruited. He was an excellent athlete. Unfortunately, he never understood the team concepts and how we wanted him to read situations that arose and make decisions on the court. He didn't see the game the way we wanted to play. He worked hard but became frustrated and froze while playing because he was thinking too much instead of just playing.

I had this problem with several players, and I should have adapted to the players rather than keep trying to get them to better understand the systems I was trying to teach. I should have given the players more freedom and less specific direction during games. What further complicates this is you have many players of all ages and abilities, both physical and mental, in the program. Some understand most of what you are teaching, others not so much. There's a basketball IQ, and some players are just smarter on the court than others. The goal is to get all the players on the court thinking as one. If one of the five is out of synch, there will be a breakdown in the process of what you want to accomplish.

Figuring out how to teach and coach the group to execute together is like working on a Rubik's cube. But this mixing of all the different personalities and skill levels helped a great deal when I became a sales rep. Buyers, store owners, and doctors also have different abilities and motivations. Some are bright and on top of their businesses, and others aren't. It's common for the family to be involved in retail and some doctor's offices. It could be the spouse, children, or both. It's hard enough to sell to only one person. Things can get complicated and challenging when other personalities and agendas get involved.

During my last season as coach, I was in the gym before practice and waited for the players to arrive as I normally did. It was quiet—no balls dribbling, no sneakers squeaking, no whistles blowing, just me alone with my thoughts. I'd always enjoyed these few moments when I could think about the upcoming practice. But on this day, I felt different. I wasn't excited and looking forward to the upcoming couple of hours. I thought I might just be tired, but these feelings stayed with me as the days passed.

**Buyers, store owners, and doctors also have different abilities and motivations. Some are bright and on top of their businesses, and others aren't.**

I stopped enjoying the routines of the coaching job. In fact, I'd always said that coaching wasn't a job; it was a dream come true. But something had changed. I realized I no longer wanted to coach, and the thought scared me. I had a position I'd always wanted and was thinking about walking away. Was I being impulsive? Was I being immature? Had I expected to be super motivated all the time and enjoy all aspects of coaching without understanding there would be some downtimes? How could I leave this after only a few years? What would I do? Over the next few weeks, I wrestled with my situation. I simply couldn't recharge myself and offer the same energy and enthusiasm I had in the past, so I decided to resign at the end of the season.

One of my great mentors was John Guthrie, the former head coach at Georgia with whom I'd stayed in contact during all the years I coached and many years after. I told him I wanted to change careers. John knew the Vice President of Converse, Joe Dean, and it just so happened that they were looking for a rep for the New Jersey territory. I interviewed with Joe, and he offered me the job.

When I took the job, I had a very different understanding of the position at Converse than what it turned out to be. I thought it would be much more of a marketing and promotion role. I thought I'd be spending my time spreading the word about Converse, seeing coaches whose teams used the product, and recruiting coaches and players who weren't under contract to Converse. I knew I'd work with pro and college basketball, football, and baseball players and attend camps and clinics. I didn't understand that there would be a significant sales responsibility. I had a rude awakening as soon as I started the job.

The Converse training program was to have a new rep travel with one of their established reps for a few days. I went to Massachusetts to spend a few days observing one of the top reps. He picked me up at the hotel early in the morning. I thought we'd have breakfast with a coach or observe a morning practice. Instead, we drove to a sporting goods store. We said hello to the owner and immediately went to the basement, where he handed me an inventory pad, something I'd never seen. We started to count all the sneakers manually. This was, of course, before barcoding and electronic systems that track inventory. Hundreds of shoes were stacked on top of each other, and this was no easy task. I was on my hands and knees moving boxes, looking for stock numbers and sizes on the boxes, and slashing units onto the inventory sheet. It was dark, dirty, and dusty, and I quickly became hot and sweaty, not having a lot of fun on my first morning on the job.

What I learned was a very basic inventory-to-order process. We recorded the on-hand inventory and proposed a fill-in order for missing or low-inventory items to the buyer. This is how an at-once order is created. We then presented some new styles of sneakers for additional orders. I observed how the shoes were presented and what information the rep offered.

When I realized half my job would be selling, I thought about the process of recruiting players and realized I'd now need to recruit store owners and buyers. I'd learned the basics of recruiting players from John Guthrie, a Georgia native and a southern gentleman. He was fun, pleasant, and upbeat and a master at building relationships with high school coaches and players. He always had a smile on his face and spoke with a pleasant southern drawl. John seemingly knew all the coaches in the state. He knew their families and what their interests were, and he knew their history of coaching. He always complimented them on their successes. Because they had a high-caliber player that interested us, the season was usually going well, so he complimented the coach for the job he was doing to develop such an outstanding player. I remembered what I'd learned from him and thought, *I'm going to recruit these buyers the same way I learned to recruit coaches and players. I'll try to learn as much as possible about their families and interests and build a personal relationship with them.*

**When I realized half my job would be selling, I thought about the process of recruiting players and realized I would now need to recruit store owners and buyers.**

My sales career started right there in that dark and dusty basement. My job description was to be a sales and marketing rep, a two-part job. Converse had a war chest of resources to help build buyer relationships and secure orders. We had 150 NBA players under contract, which meant they wore Converse on the court whenever they played and made promotional appearances. We had some of the best and most well-known players—Magic Johnson, Larry Bird, Dominique Wikens, Isiah Thomas, and Bernard King, to name just a few. We also had stars in other sports: Chris Evert and Jimmy Connors in tennis, Tony Dorsett in football, and Don Mattingly in baseball. We also had elite coaches such as Dean Smith of North Carolina; Joe B. Hall, the Kentucky Head Coach; Billy Tubbs of Oklahoma; Hubie Brown, a coach of many NBA teams; Rick Pitino, the Coach of Providence and the New York Knicks; and many others. Converse hosted all the NCAA basketball coaches at the Final Four, and we were the official shoe of both the NBA and the US Open in tennis. There were also many regional and local events in which Converse had invested to present the brand and reach consumers and buyers.

We also had tickets and VIP access to every arena and stadium. I could bring my customers and their families to games and spend time with them. On many occasions, I brought buyers *and* their children into the locker room to meet our players under contract. This was a special bonus for buyers, especially when their children could meet these major stars.

I used the resources to build the business. For example, if we wrote an order for 250 pairs of assorted sneakers, I offered to bring a professional player to the store for an appearance at no charge. However, the order had to be for four hundred pairs to do this. This was a win-win all around. The store owner would have a special event; I'd secure a bigger order, and the player would fulfill one of the required appearances in their contract. For larger customers like Macy's or Bloomingdales and national athletic chains like Footlocker, Converse provided elite athletes for their advertising and promotional events. They could plan their marketing campaigns around Converse athletes.

At one time, Converse had over 90 percent share of the sneaker market. But the company couldn't physically support the entire country. There were too many accounts, so they built a nationwide distributor network so local accounts could order from a nearby distributor. The distributor sold the same products our national sales team sold, which created some problems. We stepped on each other's toes when we went after the same accounts, which was confusing and uncomfortable for the buyers.

Very soon after, I started working in New Jersey (pre-internet, of course). I met the owner of a sizable account who had three stores and a large mail-order business. We had a lot in common. We were about the same age. He grew up in Brooklyn. He was a big sports fan, and he played basketball and tennis. When we started talking about the business, he said, "Stu, why would I order from Converse directly when I've been ordering from the distributor? I can have the sneakers the next day if I order before noon. If I order from Converse, the warehouse is in Massachusetts, and I must wait several days. Why would I order from you?"

I said, "Why not order from the distributor when you need small fill-ins the next day and order directly from me and Converse for your larger orders that you don't need so quickly, your stocking orders? Also, I will recruit you and take great care of you." I told him about all the perks I would provide.

I said, "You like tennis. Converse is the official shoe of the US Open, and I will take you and your wife to the US Open. You like basketball, so I'll get you tickets to Knicks and Nets games. You like to play tennis and basketball, so I'll play with you, and we'll become friends."

That first meeting was forty years ago, and I've been friends with Marvin Stein all these years. We played basketball and tennis together for years and now golf together regularly. I have several pictures in my office of Marvin and his wife and me when they attended receptions with Jimmy Connors and another with them with Rick Pitino. I built this same type of relationship with many buyers and store owners using Converse's many resources. We set up dinner meetings with elite athletes where buyers could bring their wives and children to meet these players. We arranged in-store events where we could promote that a pro athlete was coming to the store for a few hours. This is what I learned from Coach Guthrie about building relationships.

When I took the job, I knew nothing about the distributor network and quickly realized I was selling and competing against my brand. Converse corporate supplied the distributors with all the products, so the company was satisfied with this process. But I sure wasn't because product was coming into my territory, and I wasn't making any money on it.

I thought about how I could outsell the distributors and decided to communicate the "Converse Policy" to all my accounts. I wrote and sent a letter to all my accounts that said the Converse policy was that larger orders would be written by the local sales reps (Stu), and the local distributors would fill smaller fill-in orders. I didn't discuss my policy letter with my regional manager. I just sent it out.

It didn't take long for my phone to ring. Keep in mind that the distributors were the company's largest accounts, and when the owner of the local distributor saw the letter I'd sent, he exploded. He called Gib Ford, executive vice president of Converse. Gib had been the co-captain of the gold-medal United States Olympic basketball team. He was a southern gentleman from Texas and very strict, and here I was, rocking the boat in my first few months on the job. He told me I'd made a mistake and shouldn't have sent that letter—and to never do so again—a lesson well learned. As aggressive as I was in securing orders, I learned that there's a chain of command within an organization, and I needed to ask permission from those in management when I wanted to do something out of the box. My letter did help secure a good amount of business and let buyers know I was serious about wanting their orders. It worked out well, as I was recognized as Salesman of the Year at Converse for two consecutive years.

In the late 1970s and early 1980s, two new companies, Nike and Reebok, entered the athletic footwear business. Both companies saw the promotional and advertising formula that Converse had employed. They not only emulated signing and promoting athletes and coaches, but both companies also created innovative ways to promote these athletes with outstanding marketing campaigns. Remember "It Must Be the Shoes" with Michael Jordan and Spike Lee or "Bo Knows," featuring Bo Jackson?

Nike and Reebok changed the landscape of the athletic footwear industry. They did so in several ways, the most significant being that they spent a great deal of money signing up athletes and coaches. It wasn't uncommon for Nike and Reebok to double the dollars that Converse paid. Many players and coaches stayed with Converse due to the strong relationships we'd built, and many buyers stayed loyal to the brand and placed orders they may not have needed. They wanted to help us even though they knew the brand was fading.

Working for Converse now felt like standing at a train station watching two high-speed trains flash by while waiting for the slow train. Converse was reactionary, not innovative. One day, I walked into the Footlocker offices expecting to meet with the buyer for basketball, our strongest category. They said he was designing next year's new styles in China with Nike. I was going to show him the same new styles we'd be presenting to all other customers, large and small, while he was designing next season's shoes and placing orders in the Nike factory. That day, I knew I wasn't on the right team, and it was time to make a move.

Around this same time, I got a call from a recruiter. I'd never spoken with a recruiter before, and he asked if I'd be interested in interviewing for a shoe company that was growing fast and needed help with middle management. When he used the phrase "growing fast," I was intrigued because of what I was feeling and living at Converse.

The company was Rockport, and the open position was Eastern Regional Sales Manager. They were interested in meeting me. I didn't know much about Rockport then, so I dove into learning as much as possible.

The more I learned, the more excited I became. Rockport sounded like the Nike of the traditional shoe business. The company was innovative in that they were creating the comfort and walking categories of shoes, which at the time was groundbreaking. Bruce Katz, the owner's son, thought to use the same materials found in lightweight running shoes for conventional footwear. Long-established dress shoes were made of stiff, clunky, heavy leather. Today, comfort footwear has evolved, and consumers expect shoes to be comfortable; however, this was not the case back then. In addition to the dress category, Rockport designed lightweight shoes for this new category of shoe—the walking shoe. Consumers were responding in a big way to these new shoes, and the company was growing.

I took the position at Rockport. The company had only four regions, and the East was the largest. My first day on the job was at the summer national meeting in Newport, Rhode Island. Almost every salesperson in the region made industry-leading money because the brand was the hottest in the shoe business.

At my first meeting with my salesman, the top rep in the company raised his hand and asked if he could ask a question. He said, "We've been doubling this business every season for the last few years. We, the sales reps, have built this business. What do we need you for?"

*Wow!* What a way to start my first encounter with my team of reps.

I thought about the question and said, "Undoubtedly, each of you has done a great job in helping build the brand. My job is to work with you to get you all the company resources you need. When a company grows as fast as this one, information needs to flow in both directions, from the field to management and from management to the field. My job is to fill in that information both ways."

I went on to say, "Actions speak louder than words. None of you know me, and I don't know you. Let's do this; let's just get to work for the next few months. You'll see what I'm about and how I work, and I'll see what you're about."

We lived through the next few months, and things went well. Rockport had grown fast, and the reps didn't have anyone but the VP of Sales to chase down for information or assistance. He was swamped. That's why he hired me. I had a great group of reps to work with, and they saw that I worked to help them in any way I could. The business continued to grow, and our region did well.

I don't know where or when I heard this expression, but it's stayed with me since the day I

**"When it comes time to perform, everything leaves you except your practice."**

heard it, probably as a young player: "When it comes time to perform, everything leaves you except your practice." There are so many similarities between preparing a team and preparing to sell. In both, there's a practice period to improve skills. You study past performances and information and discover opportunities for success. There's the game and the presentation, then the post-performance evaluation.

My professional life has been a constant preparation, performance, and review cycle. To this day, I learn from those I work with. This book aims to help my sales colleagues become highly skilled sales professionals, so they can earn more money, gain more freedom, and enjoy a higher quality of life.

# 2

## ARE YOU SALES REP MATERIAL?

One of my uncles was a big sports fan, and when I decided to leave coaching and go to work for Converse, he heard about it. He was a career salesman in the paper goods business. He called and asked why I'd decided to make a career change, and then he said something I've never forgotten. I can still hear his voice in my head all these years later.

He said, "Well, Stu, you've just entered the loneliest profession there is. You're always on your own and are responsible for all that will be accomplished."

He was right. There are a lot of lonely hours on the road, and there's a lot of planning and behind-the-scenes work. Surprisingly, there isn't a lot of time in front of the customers. Since I was on my own, I created tasks for myself each day and each week to be both busy and effective, so my hours and days would be full and hopefully productive.

Here are some important questions to ask yourself if your goal is to become a highly effective, professional salesperson:

- Are you coachable?
- Are you committed?
- Are you inspired and inspiring?
- Are you a leader or a follower?
- Are you prepared?
- Are you growing or shrinking?
- Are you hungry or satisfied?
- Are you ready for the next step in your career?
- Do you have the right balance in your life?
- If you didn't show up today, would you be missed?

Let's explore each one of these questions.

## Are You Coachable?

In sales, you need to be coachable. Why? Because there are no "naturally born salespeople." It takes a lot of work and experience to become a sales professional. Like all professions, there are many skills you must acquire, and if you're openminded to be coached and learn, you'll make progress.

Salespeople are measured on many things, not just writing orders and reaching revenue goals. We're evaluated on our cold-calling abilities, how we make presentations, and how we plan the business. Sales managers will observe you and make suggestions for improvement. A good rep must set their ego aside to absorb the advice and feedback regarding their skills and take time to improve. Great coaches can be effective, but their students must put in the work to improve.

**It takes a lot of work and experience to become a sales professional.**

A while back, I helped start a first-of-its-kind medical services business. We hired experts in casting for braces that solved foot problems. It's a heavy responsibility to hold someone's foot and cast them, and then to place a brace on their foot that they hope will relieve their pain. Everyone we found for this start-up business was dedicated and experienced as technical clinicians, but none were salespeople. In their previous positions, patients came to them in a medical office. Now they traveled to doctors' offices and to see patients. The primary objective was still to cast and fit custom devices, but a new part of the job called for building revenue in these offices.

For example, if a doctor had scheduled six patients in one month and then a few months later the number of scheduled patients had slipped to three, there needed to be a conversation with the doctor or office manager about why things were moving in the wrong direction. Also, these clinicians were compensated on the number of braces they ordered, so the rep had to discover why the scheduled appointments had declined and then learn how to grow the business. I had to coach these people in basic sales techniques, which for almost all of them was uncomfortable and not what they'd been doing for many years.

Some were more receptive than others. I worked with a shy young man who was an outstanding technician, but he'd never made a cold call, shared any sell-through information, and never asked for an order. But he was motivated to grow his business.

Some of the questions I asked were:

- What do you know about this doctor and the practice? To use a basketball approach, what's the scouting report on this doctor?
- Which products do you think would be best to present?
- What are realistic goals with this practice?
- What would be a good strategy for this meeting?
- How should we share this presentation? Do you want to begin, or should I?

Over the course of a couple of years, he became more confident and took control of presentations. His business grew steadily, and he became a sales professional.

## Are You Committed?

You get out of anything the effort you put in. Some other words for committed are dedicated, compelled, and driven. To become a successful sales professional, you must be dedicated to improving and growing your basic skills.

I once hired a rep for one of our top territories. The previous rep had built a sizable business and moved on within the company. The new rep's first day happened to be at our national meeting. When everyone arrived, they received binders, folders, and a lot of material that would be reviewed during the meeting. At the first breakout session, I happened to be making the presentation. I looked out from the podium and saw this rep seated in the last row. He had nothing with him— not one piece of paper, not a pen or pencil. Everyone else had notebooks, flyers, brochures, and price lists, and they were taking notes.

**To become a successful sales professional, you must be dedicated to improving and growing your basic skills.**

It's amazing what can go through your mind while making a presentation. I thought, *Did I make a mistake in hiring this fellow? Was he committed to learning all that he needed?* As it turned out, he wasn't. In a short time, the sales in his territory started moving in the wrong direction and shrinking significantly. He voiced a lot of excuses about why the accounts weren't ordering from him.

I've often told reps that as a manager, it's not difficult to measure which reps are into it and which ones aren't. Reps often place themselves in the top, middle, or bottom of the

23

performance measurements. Over time, it becomes easy to evaluate one rep compared to the rest of the group.

## Are You Inspired and Inspiring?

To accomplish great things, a professional must be motivated to succeed. Ralph Waldo Emerson said, "Nothing great was ever achieved without enthusiasm." A related question is, "What moves you?" Inspiration comes in many forms, and you need it to achieve success. Not only must *you* be inspired, but *your customers* also want to be inspired and motivated by how the product and service are presented.

**Ralph Waldo Emerson said, "Nothing great was ever achieved without enthusiasm."**

One reason why companies have sales meetings is to rally the troops. It's lonely out there in the field, and when an organization comes together, it's important to energize everyone. Many companies bring in motivational speakers who can help build excitement and assist with the theme of the meeting. As a rep, it's important to be open to being inspired. Sometimes, we can all use a boost, and the internet is a wonderful resource for finding motivational speakers. Coaches such as Lou Holtz and Nick Saben and business leaders Bill Gates and Brian Tracy are all outstanding speakers. Many politicians are as well, like Presidents Obama and Clinton, who are inspiring and entertaining speakers.

It's important to think about customers when thinking about this subject. They can feel our enthusiasm and want to know that we believe in the company's leadership and the products we present. Our goal should be to motivate and inspire the customer. On

**Our goal should be to motivate and inspire the customer.**

several occasions following a presentation, customers have asked me if I owned the company. This is a great compliment because my enthusiasm and belief in the company came through during the meeting.

### Are You a Leader or a Follower?

Many careers don't require you to be a leader, but you must be in sales. A sales pro must take charge of the selling process and direct the buyers and others connected to the sale. Even if someone might not be a leader in other aspects of life, they must be in their sales role. Most of the outstanding salespeople I know were either leaders or they grew to be.

I worked with a rep in the south who'd played major college football. He had a wonderful personality; he was upbeat and friendly. When he walked into a presentation, he commanded everyone's attention. He knew his product, and his positive, upbeat leadership style was always well received. Buyers want to work with positive people.

### Are You Prepared?

There are no shortcuts to becoming a highly skilled sales professional. There's lots of grunt work involved. You must evaluate the opportunity, study past performance, and plan a strategy for achieving success.

I've seen both sides of this. Nothing is more embarrassing than seeing a rep who isn't on top of the needed information stumble through a presentation. Buyers work with so many salespeople, and they can quickly tell if someone doesn't have the goods or if they're not prepared. On the flip side, observing a well-prepared rep is a pleasure. They've done their homework, know the past numbers, and present confidently, and the sales call flows extremely professionally.

## Are You Growing or Shrinking?

I ask myself this question all the time. Are my skills better to-day than six months or a year ago? Of course, you want to reach a certain level of professional skill and build a foundation within yourself to be solid in your craft. But you must also continue to improve.

Some of your skills on autopilot are positive because you know you can call on them when needed. However, as the world evolves, you could get set in your ways and get behind the times. The explosion of technology provides a great example. It's very challenging and uncomfortable to use some of the new technology. Still, if you want to keep up, you need to overcome the discomfort and learn new skills that will make you more efficient and better as a professional.

## Are You Hungry or Satisfied?

Sales is a constant, daily quest to find a new customer, schedule an appointment, write an order, and make progress. It's easy to be content and satisfied in your personal life, but to be a skilled sales professional, you must always reach for more and be hungry.

## Are You Ready for the Next Step in Your Career?

Not everyone aspires to become a sales manager. But if you do, what are you doing to achieve that goal? A good first step is to tell your manager that you'd like to grow into a candidate for management. Ask what they think you need to work on to reach that goal. Be on the lookout for ways you can contribute beyond your current responsibilities. If a committee is forming or a new rep needs to be trained, step forward and do more. It will be noticed.

## Do You Have the Right Balance in Your Life?

This can be a difficult challenge because most high-achieving sales reps are driven to succeed and often place their career above all other aspects of their lives. The balance between work, family, friends, and recreation is important to keep work in perspective. Having a balance helps you perform better at work. I love the expression that on one's deathbed, no one looks back and says to themselves, "I wish I had spent more time working."

## Would You Be Missed?

Coach Nick Saban, the most successful college football coach in history, asks, "If you didn't show up today, would you be missed?" This is a fabulous question. Are you contributing to your company? Do your colleagues value your input? Would anyone notice if you weren't there? You will be missed if you're productive, contributing, and effective in your position.

## A WIN A DAY

Think about this: If you can achieve at least one win a day, you can claim at least twenty achievements at the end of the month. Certainly, you'd like to accomplish several wins a day—a new order, appointment, or customer—and you may achieve several wins on many days. But there are also many days when things are slow. There are no orders; no one returns your calls or emails, and you strike out on cold calls. These are the days that a professional will dig in and get something positive done. Just one thing, anything. On many days when it's late and it's been a slow day, I ask myself, "What can I do to get that one win?"

One Friday afternoon while at Converse, I got home and tallied up the week of orders. I was short of my goals for the week. Extra dollars were earned for writing a future order and for new categories. I knew my wife and I had plans that night, and even though it was getting late, I called a shoe store not too far from where we lived. I asked if I could come over to show some new products. The owner agreed to see me, which turned into a sizable order well beyond what I expected. I remember going out with my wife that night, feeling proud that I'd made that extra effort to accomplish my goals for the week.

> **You get a certain satisfaction on those difficult days when it's been a struggle, and something finally pops through to give you that win.**

You must keep grinding. I call it grunt work, but I want that one win before I can end my day. You get a certain satisfaction on those difficult days when it's been a struggle, and something finally pops through to give you that win.

## WHAT I LEARNED IN COACHING THAT HELPED SECURE A WIN A DAY

Like in sales, there are a lot of difficult days in coaching. The team doesn't play well, a player gets injured, or a recruit doesn't show up for a visit. Somehow you must stay positive and make progress in some way. I know my failures and difficult days in coaching helped me go after that one win a day as a sales rep. Some customers are difficult to work with, or shipments get delayed. On days like that, I'd feel the same cold sweat and stomach ache I had when coaching. So, I reminded myself what I used to tell my players: "Play through the problem. Make a positive play. Get a rebound. Draw a charge. Double team the ball. These are all ways to make something good happen."

I tried to do just that in selling. I tried to find a way to solve the problem or devise an alternative plan. If one product was backordered, I suggested a replacement, maybe with a little incentive or discount. If a product wasn't selling, I'd create a contest for the salespeople on the floor. Do what's required to make a positive play.

## FOR FURTHER THOUGHT:

- Which questions in this chapter made you feel you have what it takes to be a successful sales professional?
- Was there a question or two that had you rethinking your commitment to a sales career?
- Is there a question or two that pointed out a skill you need to work on to become a successful sales professional?
- Can you commit to a win a day?

# 3

## TAKING THE "FREEZE" OUT OF COLD CALLING

One of the greatest career challenges is to be a stand-up comedian. Imagine walking out on stage where everyone expects you to be entertaining and funny—and you only have twenty seconds to grab their attention. That takes a lot of courage and talent. When walking into cold-call situations, I've said to myself, "It's show time. Time to perform." Like a comedian, it's difficult, scary, and intimidating. At least the audience for the comedian has probably consumed some alcohol!

The last thing a receptionist probably wants to see is a salesperson coming toward her. Your challenge is to assess the situation quickly. Is the receptionist busy, friendly, stressed, or bored? Nothing is harder than when the receptionist is behind a glass window, and she must get out of her seat to slide it open, and in a cold, monotone voice, she says, "Can I help you?" Or worse, "The doctor isn't seeing any salespeople." Cold calling is always a challenge.

On many levels, cold calling basketball players and coaches is similar to cold calling store owners and doctors. The goal is to secure a meeting. The objective of the cold call is not to meet the buyer or write an order. The objective is to secure an appointment. In most cases, the gatekeeper has been directed to ward off salespeople, which makes it even harder to engage them.

> **The objective of the cold call is not to meet the buyer or write an order. The objective is to secure an appointment.**

Here's an example of what not to do: I walked into a doctor's practice and asked the gatekeeper if the office used our product and services. She quickly said that the doctor would not be interested.

I asked, "How could you know the doctor isn't interested in a service that has never existed before and that neither you nor the doctor has ever seen? Why not let the doctor decide whether to see me or not?" My tone and attitude were not very friendly because I was frustrated by her unfriendly attitude.

After that, she left the reception area, went behind a wall, waited for less than a minute, and returned and said, "The doctor is not interested."

I'm sure she never spoke with the doctor. She just wanted to get rid of me. I had created a confrontation, and the gatekeeper ended it.

I knew I'd made a big mistake in this approach and had to make some changes. I realized I had to cultivate a different mindset and game plan. I decided that gaining information from the receptionist/gatekeeper could move me toward the goal of securing a meeting with the decision maker. I also realized that, in most cases, the receptionist/gatekeeper had no authority to book an appointment. The best outcome of an encounter with the gatekeeper would be to secure information.

On future cold calls, I told the gatekeeper I was on a fact-finding mission and wasn't there to sell anything. I asked a few questions, the first of which was always, "What is your role here?" Most people like to talk about their job and what they do. Other questions were:

- How long have you worked here?
- How many patients do you see each day?
- Does the practice offer shoes or braces?

In some cases, the gatekeeper wasn't interested in having much of a conversation, but the gatekeeper became helpful and informative in more than half the cases. Some other questions I asked later in the conversation included:

- What's the best way to contact the decision maker?
- What is their email address?
- Are there designated days each week or month for appointments with reps?

Here's one of the most successful cold calls I have ever had. I was working with a new rep who was putting in the effort, but after several months, she hadn't been successful in getting appointments for presentations. I flew out to work with her for a few days. We made several cold calls early one morning and walked into a doctor's office around lunchtime. The receptionist told us the doctor was out to lunch and would return in an hour. We were already tired, having been in and out of several offices earlier in the day, but we decided to go downstairs and sit on a bench to wait for him. After forty-five minutes, we went back upstairs and stood outside the office.

A few minutes later, the elevator opened, and along came the doctor. We introduced ourselves.

He said, "I'm glad you're here because I'm having some problems with your company."

We went into his office, and he told us about his shipments and quality problems, and we told him what we would do to correct them. I then asked if I could tell him why we'd come to his office that day. We told him about the unique service we could add to his practice. When we finished, he asked if we'd come back to his city in two weeks and host a dinner for a group of doctors that he'd gathered to hear about our program. Of course, we were happy to. He told us where to book a private room and even which maître d to request to take care of us. We said we'd check back the following week to confirm that he could bring the other doctors, and then we'd book the restaurant.

We had nine doctors in a private room for dinner two weeks later. Several of them had multiple offices, and the rep had visited every one of those offices but hadn't been able to reach any of them. At the end of the presentation and dinner, eight of the nine committed to adding our program. Those eight doctors grew to over twenty locations and became the foundation for the country's highest volume territory for that program. The rep did a fabulous job servicing all the locations.

I've often asked myself what would have happened if we'd gone out for lunch when we were told the doctor was not in. By hanging out and then meeting the doctor, a great business was built for the rep and our company via that cold call.

Recently, I cold called a very busy nine-doctor office. The waiting room was packed; several patients were waiting in front of the reception desk, and all the chairs in the waiting room were full. I stood off to the side and watched the reception person or office manager at work. It was amazing how she juggled folders in one hand while speaking with patients and answering the phone—and doing it all with great efficiency.

When it finally slowed down, I said to her, "Wow, you're a superstar! I see you're swamped. I'm only here to ask if I can get an appointment with Dr. X in a couple of weeks." She asked what product we had and gave me the doctor's email address and hers. Later that day, I sent the doctor an email and copied her. No response. I sent a second email a week later, asking if the first had been seen and, again, got no response. On a Saturday morning the following week, I received an email from her that said I could come in on Tuesday or Thursday and contact her to book the appointment. I met with the doctor, and the meeting went very well. Sometimes, it takes several contacts to get an appointment.

Something that's worked well for me in selling shoes and custom medical braces is to have a product in hand as I walk in. I tell the gatekeeper, "I'm not here to sell anything; I just want to show the buyer or doctor a new product we recently added."

I always say that I only need five minutes to show them the new item. When I say I'm not there to sell anything, it seems to ease the gatekeeper's attitude and often leads to booking an appointment.

I was seeing doctors in Michigan and walked into an office holding a new brace. As I approached the receptionist, the doctor just happened to come to the front desk to drop off a patient's chart. When he saw the brace, he asked about the details, and we moved into his office for a full presentation. He placed an order. It's a rare bonus to see a doctor on a cold call.

When I was working with our rep in Arizona, we walked into a busy practice. We asked the receptionist if we could see the head doctor for a quick conversation. All the exam rooms were in a circular pattern, with several stations in the middle of the suite. She told us to stand by one of the stations and catch the doctor as he came over to enter his notes. The doctor came out, saw the brace, and booked an appointment for a couple of weeks later when all the other doctors in the practice could attend. This practice became our largest account in Arizona for that product. They don't always happen, but these positive results inspire me to keep walking in and cold calling.

Cold calling is a numbers game. The more calls you make, the more opportunities you have to eventually secure an appointment and meet with the decision makers. Try setting a daily goal for the number of walk ins or calls you make. Sometimes, I dedicate a full day to making cold calls, and sometimes, I include cold calls while I'm in the area working with other accounts. A full day of cold calling can be spiritually challenging, so combining cold calls around firm appointments works better for me. Some calls go better than others, and when you have a goal for the day, it helps deal with the ones that don't go as well.

I now have a much better attitude about cold calling and have realistic expectations for what can be accomplished. I've also found that I must be in a positive, upbeat mood. Things never go well if I walk in when I'm tired or just going through the motions. However, if I pump myself up and get excited for the opportunity to connect and uncover a good account, things go much better. For one program I was selling, one custom brace a week would generate a net profit to the doctor of $1,000. For fifty weeks, that's $50,000! Before I walked into the cold call, I thought to myself that I had a check for the doctor for $50,000. This motivated me to be excited about my conversation with the gatekeeper, and my enthusiasm shone through.

## A WIN A DAY

Occasionally a cold call leads to a meeting on the spot with the decision maker; however, that's rare. Securing information is a more realistic goal that can lead to an appointment. Connecting with the staff can be a bonus for immediate and future insights.

## WHAT I LEARNED IN COACHING THAT HELPED SECURE A WIN A DAY

In coaching, a very important part of the job is recruiting players. Recruiting is selling your university and basketball program. In most cases, the player's parents and coach—and often some advisers—are also a part of the process. Keep in mind that these are young people, seventeen-year-olds. In many cases, you see these players in gyms, parks, or camps without much time to make an impression. Somehow, in some way, you must connect with him. You must be upbeat and have an elevator speech that will interest him. After a game, there are sometimes several coaches waiting outside the locker room who want to chat with the same player you want to speak with. The player may just go down the line and speak to each coach.

This was great experience for cold calling as a rep because it required quick thinking and a brief message to try to build a first step with the player.

I always tried to find the player's parents if they were there. I knew that after a player had spoken with several coaches, he'd finish and go home with his parents. I was recruiting one of the top high school players in New York City as an assistant coach at the University of Georgia. I met his mother, and after a game, I drove her and the player home—which may have been an NCAA violation. But it went a long way toward building a relationship with both the mom and the player, and yes, he signed with us.

## FOR FURTHER THOUGHT:

- What's a good mindset to have when cold calling?
- What are some effective ways to succeed with the gatekeeper?
- What strategies and tactics have you found effective for successful cold calls?

# 4

## GOING UP AGAINST THE BIG BOYS AND WINNING

**T**here are few endeavors as competitive as recruiting players. There are so many attractive universities and basketball programs. What can be done to stand out and distance one program from all the others? One key learning was that different players are attracted to and interested in different things. Players who live in urban areas are often interested in suburban settings; players from the country are typically interested in the city.

In some cases, you never really know why a player might be attracted to your school. I asked one top recruit I signed for the University of Georgia what appealed to him to sign with us. He said he always wanted to go to school in the south, and while many schools in the northeast heavily recruited him, ours was the only one in the south that recruited him. Here I thought I'd done a great job of recruiting him, and his decision was based on our location.

When competing against other companies, I only concerned myself with what my company had to offer. I never said a negative word about a competitor and kept in mind that every company has strengths, differences, and advantages.

At one time, Converse had a 90 percent share of the sneaker market with little competition. In fact, Converse had to set up a network of distributors all around the country to be able to service all the accounts. Retailers could buy Converse from both the company directly and a local distributor. This was before Nike, Reebok, and many other companies entered the athletic-shoe world.

Three major events lined up to change the athletic footwear business. They were the emergence of Nordstrom as a national department store, women starting to purchase athletic shoes, and the national growth of fitness and running.

**Three major events lined up to change the athletic footwear business. They were the emergence of Nordstrom as a national department store, women starting to purchase athletic shoes, and the national growth of fitness and running.**

The Nordstrom family were originally shoe retailers, and when they opened their first department store in Seattle, they presented their shoe department on the first floor at a prime location. All other department stores sold very few if any, shoes, and the shoe department was often buried deep within the store, never in a prominent location. Nordstrom began to grow rapidly and became the model for all department stores with industry-leading sales per square foot.

Other department stores studied Nordstrom's assortment of products and store layouts. Who shops in department stores? Women. Most women love shoes. On average, women purchase six pairs of shoes for every pair a man buys.

At this same time, Reebok and Nike came with stylish athletic shoes, which appealed to women now participating in running and fitness. Think of your grandmothers and women of the 1950s and 60s. Women did not work out or wear athletic apparel. My mother was an outstanding athlete but wore a dress daily and never wore sneakers. Women were now purchasing athletic footwear, and the market grew dramatically. New brands like LA Gear, Skechers, Brooks, Asics, Reebok, and the granddaddy of them all—Nike—all became major companies. These brands were stylish and appealed to women; they were comfortable and cool looking. All these factors combined to change the footwear business and impact Converse in a very big way.

Converse continued to sell their iconic All-Star basketball shoe to men for playing basketball, while Nike and Reebok sold six pair or more to that fellow's wife. For a man, a shoe is a tool to play ball in. For a woman, a shoe is an accessory to her outfit. If she's wearing a black and yellow athletic outfit, she needs a shoe that goes well with it. Most women buy athletic shoes for each color of the outfits in their wardrobe.

Nike and Reebok had explosive growth in more than women's categories. They also moved into the biggest athletic footwear category: basketball. Converse had to protect its core basketball business and make some financial decisions because Nike and Reebok had grown quickly and were flush with cash.

A big part of marketing the brands was endorsement contracts with star athletes and college basketball coaches. Nike and Reebok paid these spokesmen a great deal more than Converse had been paying. At one time, Converse had over 150 NBA players under contract. To compete, Converse reduced the number of players they paid, so they could pay the top players much more than in the past. National marketing campaigns replaced most regional programs. Converse did maintain its core basketball business and tried to move into the emerging categories of running and tennis with some success, particularly in tennis with the Jimmy Connors shoe.

As the director of national accounts at Converse, I brainstormed with the VP of marketing about how we could leverage our unique sponsorship as the official shoe of the NBA. We created a special line of sneakers exclusively for Footlocker with a slide-in logo on the sneaker for every team in the NBA. The sneaker could be sold in all Footlocker stores, and any team logo could be added to the shoe. This exclusive program became a big business for Footlocker and Converse.

As formidable as Nike and Reebok were, there were lessons and strategies learned. Every company has strengths and resources it offers the customer. Converse corporate made decisions that I had to overcome for my personal success. I had to look at each retailer and find where the opportunities were to secure orders. We had some resources, such as tickets to games and events, and we could bring star players to the stores for appearances. I had to work harder for the businesses and recruit the retailer the same way I'd been taught to recruit players. Sometimes, it felt like I was buying the business, but you do what you have to in order to get the orders. Sometimes, I offered to guarantee a percentage of the sales, meaning that if they ordered the shoes, I would take some back at the end of a season if an agreed-upon percentage had not sold. That guarantee can become a problem because some retailers would then know that such an option existed and would ask for it in the future, so deciding who to offer that to was a tricky decision.

**Every company has strengths and resources it offers the customer.**

It was important to learn all the technical features and benefits of the products, all the materials that went into the shoes, and what they provided to the consumer. Selling to doctors was even more demanding because the doctor needed to know the information to present to the patient. I also had to know the retail numbers. Buyers spend a lot of analysis on the

41

dollars they have to invest, which items they decide to purchase, and how the product performs. A rep must learn about open-to-buy dollars, sell-through percentages, inventory turns, and the return on investment. How did one company's financial performance compare to another?

And then there are markdowns. What is the bottom-line contribution for each product? A major brand with a lot of advertising may have to be put on sale, while a brand that doesn't advertise as much may be able to be sold at closer to full price. It's not uncommon for a smaller brand to be more profitable than a more well-known brand.

There's an interesting phenomenon regarding retailers, brand assortment, and purchasing. Retailers certainly want to sell an emerging brand and ride the wave and sell a lot of products. However, when a brand becomes too dominant, the retailer has concerns about having too large a percentage of their open-to-buy dollars and overall business attached to only one or two brands. It's very risky if the brand starts to slow and too large a percentage of the inventory is invested in that once-hot brand. Secondary brands are an insurance policy for the retailer, and there are open-to-buy dollars still available. Also, the consumer wants choices.

Nike and Reebok challenged Converse to compete and survive, and the company did grow and improve in many ways. The product and marketing improved, and new categories like running, walking, and women's shoes were added. So, competition is a good thing because it requires a company to up their game and improve. Converse hung on for a while. However, due to many factors, the company eventually went bankrupt. Nike purchased Converse and has revived the brand in recent years, and Converse is doing very well these days.

## A WIN A DAY

When working in the medical device industry, doctors usually order from one company, and it's difficult to displace a resource that a doctor likes. To get a doctor to change companies or add a new one means you must get the doctor and staff educated and interested in providing the devices. A win would be getting an in-service or meeting to review the features and benefits. The next win would be for the doctor to schedule patients and then order the product. The final win is when the doctor receives Medicare or a private insurance company payment. This multi-step process could take several months, so it requires staying in touch regularly.

Another win relative to going up against formidable competitors is when you displace a brand, secure more styles, or add categories that you couldn't in the past. You could attend several medical conferences and have the opportunity to speak to doctors about new programs, services, and products. It's a significant win when your company is selected as a featured presenter. These speaking engagements elevate the company and provide pre- and post-meeting marketing opportunities to contact the doctors for potential presentations.

It's difficult to sell against competitors with more resources and a stronger brand, but there are ways to succeed and prosper. Every brand and company has its strengths, and the goal is to construct a plan for each customer and work hard to be a trusted advisor.

## WHAT I LEARNED IN COACHING THAT HELPED SECURE A WIN A DAY

It takes a great deal of planning and strategy to coach basketball. Some questions for an upcoming game are:

A WIN A DAY

- How is this opponent trending?
- What is their record over the last five games?
- Who are their top players, and what do these players contribute? Identify top scorers, top rebounders, and best shooters.
- How does this team like to play—fast or slow? Do they pressure?
- What does this opponent do well, and how must we prepare and execute during the game?
- What are our keys to success for this opponent?

Planning for a sales call is like preparing for a game. I can hear John O'Neil, the former President of Converse, say, "Plan your work and work your plan." A good first step is to research the customer's past performance.

- What products are selling well, which aren't, and why?
- What are my company's best products for this customer?
- What new products can be added?

**I can hear John O'Neil, the former President of Converse, say, "Plan your work and work your plan."**

- What resources or support do we need to provide to this customer?

## FOR FURTHER THOUGHT:

- What did you learn about how to compete against formidable competition?
- Why are there always opportunities for quality products, no matter the competition?
- How have you had success when selling against top competitors?

# 5

---

# PRICING OBJECTIONS

rice is often a buyer's first objection. For some, price is the single most significant factor, and figuring out its importance is critical to moving toward a sale. Some buyers throw the price issue on the table early without the benefit of hearing your full presentation. Others will wait to hear what you say and then talk pricing. In all cases, you want to be able to finish your presentation so they'll understand the product benefits before learning the costs.

Probably the most recognized retailer for low-priced items is Walmart. As Walmart emerged as a national brand in the early 1980s, I became Converse's national accounts director. Our President, John O'Neil, and I went to the Walmart headquarters in Bentonville, Arkansas. Mr. O'Neil had started working on the Converse factory floor in New England and rose through the ranks to become president. He was a patient and kind senior executive, always willing to help with any customer. Walmart always promoted low prices and emphasized their priority for Made in America products within the stores. We thought we had a good chance to do business with them. Converse had the largest footwear factory in the United States in Lumberton, North Carolina, where the well-known Converse Canvas All Star was manufactured. The All Star had a fairly low cost, and it was made in the US by a large Native American workforce.

Much has been written about Walmart and how frugal they can be, and we sure got a taste of it when visiting their offices in Arkansas. I couldn't believe the condition of their headquarters. While walking to the buyer's office, our shoes stuck to the cracked and faded linoleum. The meeting room felt like a cheap trailer parked on the side of the road to sell fruit and vegetables or tire rims. The only thing missing was fly paper hanging from the ceiling. We understood that the company wanted to save as much money as possible to pass along low prices to their customers; however, this setup was an embarrassment and quite uncomfortable. When we left, all I wanted to do was take a hot shower. I would have thought that they would have shown the president of a major company a little more respect.

The two of us sat in cheap plastic chairs, and we put our shoe samples on an uneven, stained, and rickety card table. The only thing the buyer asked was how low we would go on price. He asked if we could manufacture a less expensive version of the famous All Star. He quickly moved past our emphasis on the fact that unlike any other sneaker they could have in the stores, Converse was well-known and a Made in America brand. The buyer didn't care about anything but the price. We told him we'd research manufacturing a less expensive All Star. We both knew we'd never sacrifice the quality of the shoe to reach a reduced cost. We left frustrated because the singular focus was on the price rather than all the marketing and planning we'd contribute to building a significant presence within their stores. Walmart could have benefitted from one of the most recognizable brands in the world, and we could have generated a great deal of revenue, but that was not meant to be.

Sometimes you cannot get to a price that works for both companies. A couple of responses to price objection are: "If we put the pricing off to the side, is this a product or service you would want to purchase?" If yes, "Where would we need to be price wise for you to place an order?"

Sometimes there could be a discount for the customer, maybe not depending on the product or service. In some cases, explaining the company's margins can put things in perspective. For example, custom orthotics and custom braces have very low margins. Custom-made means they're made one at a time with high labor costs. When selling to doctors, some asked for a discount, but when they learned how low our margins were, they appreciated that information and often moved away from the pricing objection. Some buyers appreciated that information, and some didn't care.

**"If we put the pricing off to the side, is this a product or service you would want to purchase?"**

Some people always want to negotiate. It's in their DNA. I was selling Converse to a multi-location sporting goods chain that had been around for many years. They had a reputation for low pricing. Converse had never wanted to sell to this customer because of their low-price reputation. It just so happened that my brother's childhood best friend became the vice president of this company, and I knew I could get a meeting with him. But first, I had to get approval from senior management to sell to this retailer, which I did. My brother's friend and the company's owner sat in the meeting with the buyer.

The owner was super aggressive and took over the meeting. While he acknowledged that Converse represented an opportunity for the stores to bring in an established and well-known brand, all he talked about was the need for low pricing. We did have some leverage because they wanted the brand, but they were very firm on wanting a significant discount to get started.

The timing worked out for the first order because we offered a discount on the size and assortment they wanted. The prob-lem arose with the next season's

**Some people always want to negotiate. It's in their DNA.**

order. We no longer offered the same discount program. I knew that price would be a major fac-tor in placing new products.

I devised a plan to create a different price list for this customer that showed inflated prices. When I presented the products and prices, they asked for a discount. I told them I would see what I could do. I contacted them a few days later and said we could reduce the prices by the amount of the inflated percentage I'd added. This was pre-internet when there wasn't a lot of access to information. I mentioned my made-up discount program to my manager, who told me that what I'd done was unacceptable and could even be illegal, so that was the last time I could offer the "Stu Discount Program." The good news was that I secured an order for that second season.

Most major brands have large marketing budgets that can be used to offset the price negotiation. It's important to most customers for their vendors to provide advertising and pro-motional support (dollars), which should lead to sell-through. Converse, Rockport, and Timberland all had CO-OP adver-tising programs. These programs provide advertising dollars to the account based on the total dollars they purchased. A per-centage is established that could be used for advertising, and the company would match the dollars spent by the customer, hence the term cooperative (CO-OP) or shared dollars. In most cases, the level of the CO-OP program was established the prior year. If the CO-OP dollars earned were $5,000, the company would match the $5,000 that the customer spent for a total of $10,000 that could be spent on agreed-upon advertising.

One way to overcome a price hurdle is to offer some addi-tional dollars in the CO-OP formula and some dollars above and beyond the CO-OP funds. Advertising and marketing dollars are a key resource to negotiate around pricing objections. When the price is being discussed, a good question to ask is, "What else can we do, beyond the price, to gain your business and secure this order?" Another good option can be to invest some money into a contest for the employees. This is a win-win for the store and the company. A program where the employees can earn money based on how many of the products they sell motivates the employees to learn about the product and boosts sell-through.

**Advertising and marketing dollars are a key resource to negotiate around pricing objections.**

I was selling a service for custom-made foot braces, and the net profit to the doctor when reimbursed from Medicare was $1,400 per case. Some doctors asked for a discount, and I handled it two ways. I responded that we never knew how many braces an office would order, so we couldn't start an office with a discount. But we would evaluate the order rate after six months and then have a conversation to establish reasonable goals to secure a discount. This response was well received and seemed fair to both parties, ours and the doctors.

Sometimes, I would just move on from the price objection and get back to it. I've been known to say, "Let's get back to the price later. Let me present some additional information," hoping that the additional features and benefits will overcome the price objection.

## A WIN A DAY

A good day's win could be having a successful call or meeting with a buyer that doesn't get stuck on the pricing issues where you provide resources beyond price that can lead to a sale.

49

## WHAT I LEARNED IN COACHING THAT HELPED SECURE A WIN A DAY

In coaching, I learned that I needed to be flexible at the appropriate times and develop alternative solutions when needed. This applied to both players and in-game adjustments. Some players needed to be dealt with firmly, while others were more sensitive and needed a softer approach. I frequently had to adjust during a game to move us in the right direction.

For the buyer fixated on price, I had to come up with options that could lead to an order, just like making in-game adjustments.

## FOR FURTHER THOUGHT:

- What is an effective response when a prospect asks for a discount?
- What resources can you provide beyond discounts?
- What are some of your best tactics to overcome pricing objections?

# 6

## BUILDING CREDIBILITY

**W**hen starting a new business or service, it's crucial to establish credibility. After all, you're asking someone to buy into a new concept. It helps if you have a track record in the business and have worked with the buyer on previous concepts. However, it's more challenging when presenting a new business to someone who doesn't know you and hasn't purchased from you. For both types of targets, it's important to share the vision, present the thinking behind this new program, and clearly state what problem it solves and why it will benefit them and their customers. Some people are wait-and-see types; others are open to trying something new.

I was presenting a new program that had been very well received and was already a couple of years off the ground to a doctor. This doctor said, "Stu, I don't want to be a trailblazer."

And I told him, "Doc, with all due respect, the caboose is long out of the train station. There's no trailblazing on this. The program is up and running and is successful."

Many of the doctors I worked with were cautious and wanted to know which colleagues were already using the programs and products I sold. In the case of the doctor who didn't want to be a trailblazer, he added the program when I told him it had already been successful.

Asking questions, questions, and more questions is the path to establishing credibility with the customer. It shows you're interested in learning about their business. I try to have a few insightful, specific questions to ask a buyer about their business—relevant questions that show the buyer I did some homework and wanted to learn about their business.

**Asking questions, questions, and more questions is the path to establishing credibility with the customer.**

My first question is often, "Can you tell me a little about your business?" There have been some surprising responses to this question, some that were far removed from the basics of the business.

One doctor responded, "You want to know about my business? Well, my wife was sleeping with my partner, and I no longer have either."

That answer took my breath away and was hard to recover from. I think I said something like, "I think I forgot a sample I need to get from the car. I'll be right back." I needed a pause after that one.

People usually want to talk about their business, and you learn a lot from their answers. They talk about their journey, what they want to present to their customers, their plans, their struggles, and how you might be able to help them.

Other good questions are:

- *Who is your target customer?* Their answer lets you think about and present how to best work for this customer to serve their target customers.

- *What do you know about our company?* I like this question because a good percentage of buyers respond with some positives about our company, brand, and products—which is good. After all, it comes from them rather than from me. I can also learn what they don't know about the company or product by what they didn't include in their response.
- *How can I earn your business?* Their response tells me what I need to do. When I worked for Converse, one buyer told me, "I'm a Dallas Cowboys fan, and I want tickets to the Giants-Cowboys game." He received the tickets, and I received sizable orders.
- *Are there any other decision makers? What are their roles?* Learning who has a vote to go forward and purchase as early as possible is important.
- *What's your budget?* Their budget is critical to find out, so you can present a realistic order that fits their budget.
- *What are your expectations for our product or service?* It's important to learn if the customer has realistic expectations for what we provide. When I was selling products reimbursed from Medicare, the doctors often asked if we would guarantee they'd be paid, which we could not. There were also some questions about whether we or their office staff would submit the information to Medicare or other insurance companies. These questions or expectations came up very often, so I made them part of the presentation. Even when I included this important information, some doctors still had unrealistic expectations for what we did and did not provide.
- *Who has your business now?* In many cases, I learned about suppliers that I didn't know the customer was working with.

- *What do you like and what do you dislike about your current supplier?* I loved this question because it allowed me to compare my company's strengths against a current supplier's weaknesses.
- *What's the most important factor in your decision to purchase?* Sometimes price is a factor, and sometimes other priorities are shared, which I could respond to.
- *What can my company or service improve or add to your company?* This can be a positive response because the customer is considering why adding my company's product could improve their business.

It's also critical to be a good listener when establishing credibility. Once you ask a question, wait for an answer. Never speak after you have asked a question. Do not break the silence, no matter how long it takes for the buyer to respond.

**Never speak after you have asked a question. Do not break the silence, no matter how long it takes for the buyer to respond.**

I was selling a program that most doctors weren't using because they feared they'd be audited. Most people don't know that when doctors submit for reimbursement from Medicare, the government can revisit medical records for several years after payment has been sent. Sometimes, they contact the doctor and call for the money to be returned. The repayment always tacks on interest and, in some cases, a fine. If a doctor has been paid for several hundred devices over several years, the reimbursement could easily be hundreds of thousands of dollars. Their apprehension and fear are real and often a key reason some doctors don't offer some products to their patients.

It takes a lot of trust and credibility to influence doctors to start these programs, and it's a long start up. We provided as much information as possible. We even reviewed all the forms and documents before they were submitted in many cases, so the submissions would be correct, and the doctor would be paid. I suggested they only do a few cases initially, so the doctor would receive the reimbursements. The best-case scenario would be for payments to be received in sixty days.

Keep in mind, we billed practices as soon as we shipped the products, usually with thirty-day terms. So, the doctor had to pay for the products before the government paid him or her. We also had other doctors who were already using the programs and products available to speak with prospective doctors, and they would provide the patient notes for successfully paid documentation.

It's important to provide clear information and ask questions that confirm the buyer's understanding of the information you present. Customers want to purchase from someone they respect and can rely on. They also want to work with someone they like and trust who can demonstrate that the product, program, or service will succeed. Another way to establish credibility is to follow up quickly with any information requested during the presentation. This can be sharing a product sample or answering a technical question. Following up as soon as possible shows the buyer you're reliable, professional, and serious about building the business with them.

**Customers want to purchase from someone they respect and can rely on.**

Buyers want to know about others you're working with. It gives them more confidence when you present examples of success. Of course, you need to be discreet when mentioning the names of other customers. You don't want to be a name dropper, but when you have well-known and successful customers, including them in the presentation is very effective. There's a way to discreetly weave examples of other customers into presentations and real-life scenarios of successes. This must be done carefully. I often say, "I'm careful about mentioning who we're working with."

In addition to asking questions, I learned to prepare and present features and benefits. This is an effective style of selling. First, describe the product in detail and then list what each element provides.

Here's an example. "Here's a new brace for patients at risk for falling. It's a custom product manufactured from a scan or mold of the foot, so it fits the exact measurements and design of the patient's foot to be most secure and effective. It's lightweight and has Velcro closures, which make it easy for the patient to put on."

## A WIN A DAY

The ultimate win is securing an order and building an ongoing working relationship with the customer. Additionally, when a customer refers others with an endorsement, I knew I'd established credibility with them. When a customer asked me to train their staff, that also showed they had confidence in my understanding of their business and how I could help them.

## WHAT I LEARNED IN COACHING THAT HELPED SECURE A WIN A DAY

I had role models in coaching who I emulated in recruiting and working with players and coaches. I loved Athens, Georgia, and the university, and I thought Pace University was a fabulous school. I believed in both schools, and my enthusiasm and belief in both institutions came through in my recruiting. Applying this to sales, I always felt fortunate to believe in the products I was selling. Converse, Rockport, and Timberland were each global brands with something special to offer the consumer, and my enthusiasm and product knowledge came through to the buyers. I had the same beliefs in the medical devices and programs I presented to doctors.

## FOR FURTHER THOUGHT:

- How does asking questions help establish credibility?
- Effectively presenting features and benefits points out the best characteristics of a product or service. Practice presenting some features and benefits of your products.

# 7

## SECURING THE ORDER

In some sale situations, securing an order on the spot is expected and understood by the buyer. However, the buyer needs time to generate an order in other cases. The more information and assistance we provide to that buyer can help secure the order. Remember the questions I offered you in the last chapter? If possible, I try to find out what the process is for the buyer, who else may be involved in the decision, what information they may need, and, most significantly, the time-frame in which the order will be received.

In many cases, the buyer needs approval to issue the order. Other vendors also make presentations, and the buyer must evaluate which products they want to order from what companies. A good way to help the buyer is to present a suggested prewritten order. You can do your research into the history and performance and offer them a reasonable suggested order.

Nike changed the athletic footwear business by introducing "futures orders." Historically, store owners and buyers purchased footwear as needed, called "at once" orders. When inventory was low, buyers sent in "fill-in orders" to restock or fill in their inventory. Nike's business grew at historic levels—by hundreds of millions of dollars each season—which created major cash flow problems for them. They came up with the idea of selling orders many months in advance for the following season and included an incentive or discount on these orders. These future orders had to be received on or before a cut-off date to receive the discount.

This deadline motivated the buyers to turn in their orders. The size of the order and the types of products ordered earned a discount. For example, a 250-pair order might receive a 3 percent discount, and a 300-pair order might receive a 4 percent discount. If the order contained a minimum number of shoes in a category that hadn't been ordered before, they received an additional discount on the entire order. The incentives on future orders helped build larger orders and secure orders in new products and categories.

Other manufacturers copied this strategy. As a major player in the basketball category, Converse wanted to branch out into running, tennis, and cleated shoes. We had future incentives that earned significant discounts for each new category the account ordered. The reps were also incentivized. On one future program, if the total number of shoes were ordered, there was an earned dollar figure. And for every new category booked, there were additional dollars.

I set daily and weekly goals to write x number of those future orders. The requirements for the incentives for the buyer were somewhat confusing—just about every company had these future programs, and they all had different requirements. I found I could assist the buyer by providing a suggested pre-written order. This was helpful in several ways. Buyers can be very busy, and helping them is often welcomed.

In many cases, evaluating inventory, turn, ROI, and margin is part of the rep's job. The buyer has many companies and products to consider. Buyers are incentivized and penalized for the sell-through and margins on the products they buy. A rep must understand these factors and work with the buyer on orders that make the best sense to accomplish sell-through.

Some sales call for a contract to add a service or program. It's rare for the agreement to be signed immediately after **Whenever applicable, I** the presentation as there are **always present a buyer** legal aspects to the agreement **with a suggested** that the buyer needs to have **order. This is helpful** reviewed and approved by **in several ways.** upper management or their attorney.

In many instances, I've had to wait a long time to secure an order or agreement, especially when working with doctors. I once presented a medical device product, and for three years in a row, I saw this successful doctor at an annual conference. I reminded him how effective the product was each year and what a sizable financial opportunity it could be for his practice.

Just after the start of the fourth year, he called and said, "Stu, you owe me $100,000."

I said, "What are you talking about?"

He said, "My younger associates have started to order that product, and it's going very well. But you should have pushed me harder to get on board with it because I could have been making a lot of money these last few years."

He was kidding, of course, but it's a good example of how long it can sometimes take.

During presentations, I always ask who else will be a part of the decision and what the timing might be. Some of the programs I've sold take time for the decision to be made, and sometimes the buyer has second thoughts and must be sold again or be reminded why they were interested in the first place. Presenting the information several times gets frustrating, but that's part of the job.

Think about your last car-buying experience. You were probably asked many questions: How much do you drive monthly? What type of car do you currently drive? What are you looking for in your next vehicle? What do you do for a living? The car salesman is trying to learn as much as possible to find a car that matches what you're shopping for. Asking effective questions is always a good path to securing an order.

**During presentations, I always ask who else will be a part of the decision and what the timing might be.**

We've all been in a car dealership and had the manager ask, "What will it take to get you into this car today?" That's a good question. It gets right to the key objections or concerns the buyer has. People categorize car salespeople negatively, which I think is unfair. I greatly respect how informed most car salespeople are and the long hours they put into work in their field. As a profession, car dealerships invest a lot of money in training and sales skills. The purchase of a car is often the second largest investment someone makes after their home. We can learn a lot from this industry regarding sales skills.

I once worked for Dr. Sheldon Langer, the Founder of Langer Labs. Dr. Langer worked as a drug rep, then returned to school to become a podiatrist. He was super entrepreneurial and a marketing genius. He was always coming up with new and innovative products and programs. I joined his company from the shoe business, and we presented a program for doctors that few had brought to their offices. Dr. Langer and I went to several conferences together, and it became frustrating because of how long it took these doctors to decide to add or, worse, pass on the program. Dr. Langer told me about a doctor who stood in the back of the audience the first year, moved to the next-to-last row the year after, and by the fourth year, he finally moved to the front of the group and was ready to add the system. It takes some people a long time to decide.

As a rep for Converse, there was a large multi-location store called Shoetown. They had seventy stores. Converse had never worked with this retailer because the stores were all self-service with lower-end brands. The buyer was an old shoe dog. I met with him several times and felt the momentum was building toward an order, and I secured approval from Converse management to pursue an order. I had an appointment with the buyer in March to pick up the order.

When I woke up the morning of the appointment, a snowstorm pelted against the window. I decided to make my way over to the buying office anyway. I didn't know if the buyer would even be in the office because he lived in the middle of the state, which was a good drive away. I slowly drove through the snow, and when I arrived, only a few cars were in the parking lot. The waiting room, usually packed with reps, was empty, and there was no receptionist there. So, I sat down and waited.

About an hour later, I heard the downstairs door slam, and whoever it was stomped their feet to remove the snow and walked slowly up the staircase. I saw the top of the buyer's head, and when he saw me, he shook his head and said, "I had a feeling you'd be here. Come back to my office, and let's finish this order." I left with one of the largest orders Converse had ever received as a first order, and it was for thousands of shoes.

**You do what you have to do.**

You do what you have to do. Driving through the snow was not how I secured the order. I first had to sell Converse senior management to get the approval to sell to the customer, and then I stayed on top of the buyer for several months. When I left the office, the snow had stopped. The sun was out, and it was a great day.

You must be certain that you're presenting to the person who can make the buying decision. In some instances, someone might have the title of *buyer*, but in reality, they're only gathering information to present to the one with the authority to buy. You must still go through the command chain and work with this intermediary person. It can get tricky because you really want to work directly with the key person. Over time, you can build toward that; however, at the start, you usually have to play it out, dance to their tune, and follow their process.

There are also times when it makes sense to walk away and not pursue an order. I've walked into retail and medical businesses and decided that, for various reasons, it wouldn't make sense to move ahead. I've passed on retailers who wouldn't present the brand with at least a minimum of the recommended assortment and were only cherry-picking an item or two. I've also stayed away from retailers who would significantly discount the product and cause problems for other customers in the market.

When I worked at Rockport and Timberland, the brands were growing fast, and we were getting placement in some new distribution channels like department stores and better women's shoe stores. I had to decide which retailers to sell to based on several factors. One was the image of the retailer in the marketplace. If we were just starting with a department store, we didn't want to be in a hunting and fishing store right up the street. I had to negotiate with that hunting and fishing retailer to raise their price and present the brand differently. Because there was limited inventory, we could also direct the product to the type of stores we wanted to be in.

When I was placing medical devices inside doctors' offices, the decision not to work with some was often based on the inefficiency of their staff and the doctor's poor business skills. Most doctors want to be good at taking care of their patients. In fairness, they get little training about how to run a business, which is a problem for them and the companies that want to sell to them. In every medical company I've worked for, we spent a tremendous amount of time, energy, and money teaching doctors and their staff how to organize their practice, create and keep track of performance vs. goals for the products, and what codes to submit to Medicare and private insurance companies for reimbursement. There's a lot for an office staff to handle, and most do a decent job. But I've met with some, and I could see that the doctor and his staff couldn't grasp all that was needed. I knew that no matter how hard I tried to help them, they would never get it. Working with these types of practices is a huge drain on time and energy, and it makes sense to walk away. In some cases, you can't walk away because the account is already a customer or because the account has a sizable business.

A big key is the staff. When I walk into an office and learn that the office manager has been there for fifteen or twenty years, and I observe a well-run practice, there's a good chance I can make progress. On the flip side, when there's constant staff turnover, it's a red flag that this doctor doesn't know how to run a business, and it might make sense not to get involved. In my unscientific calculation, I would say that at least 50 percent of the doctors I've worked with are poor businesspeople. They are dedicated to their patients, but they'd be wise to either invest some time learning the basics of running a business or bring in a business professional.

**I've learned that in sales, you never have more leverage than before you start.**

I've learned that in sales, you never have more leverage than before you start. Once you take that first order, you're connected to that account, and it's difficult to shut them down if they aren't presenting the brand how you want them to. As difficult as it might be, you must set some ground rules and objectives so you have a chance for success. If a retailer understands what the brand is trying to convey and will market and merchandise it in the way that you are looking for, things should go well.

Selling to doctors is much more complicated than selling to retailers. Doctors do not want to be perceived as salespeople, which is understandable. The best doctors I've worked with never discuss prices with their patients. They present the features and benefits of a product and let the patient decide. If the patient has questions about price, the doctor tells them the staff will answer them. It's important that the doctor believes in the product and enthusiastically recommends it. Custom orthotics are one example where the doctor should not be discussing price. The doctor should educate the patient that the foot's function can be corrected with a custom device made from a mold of their foot that will help relieve any discomfort or condition they're experiencing.

Many doctors could never get comfortable learning how to present products to their patients. We offered them scripts of exactly what to say to their patients. Some made some progress; most did not. In fairness to the doctors, the Internet has made their presentation of some products more difficult because patients can purchase shoes, inserts, and even braces online. In some cases, the same product that the doctor provides can be purchased for less cost via the Internet. This can be an uncomfortable situation for the doctor. He or she is paying staff, overhead, and many expenses that the internet business doesn't incur. The doctor could either decide to match the price on the Internet or stop selling products offered online.

## A WIN A DAY

The best win would be to secure the order, but there are other small wins that indicate that things are moving in the right direction. A call or email from the prospect who asks a question about any aspect of the order is a good sign that an order is still being considered.

## WHAT I LEARNED IN COACHING THAT HELPED SECURE A WIN A DAY

Recruiting a player always takes several months; sometimes, it can take years. There are times when it feels like a player is interested, and then for several reasons, the player can become less interested. The best learning was to be patient and consistent and stay in touch with him. You read about some heavily recruited players being called or communicated daily for months. To me, that's way too often and an inconvenience to the player and his family.

**I call it professional persistence. I have a once-a-week rule to stay in touch with a buyer about an order.**

Be patient. I call it professional persistence. I have a once-a-week rule to stay in touch with a buyer about an order. One contact a week—a call, email, text message, or even a drop-in visit. Each contact should deliver a different type of message, such as, "Do you need any additional information," "I'm just checking in," "Have you made a decision?" or "What can I do for you at this time?"

## FOR FURTHER THOUGHT:

- What key information must you know to move toward securing an order?
- What are some effective ways to move the buyer to provide the order?
- Why is presenting the buyer with a suggested order a good idea?
- Why might it make sense to not work with a customer?

# 8

## OVERCOMING FEAR, REJECTION, FAILURE, BOREDOM, AND LONELINESS

've read the statistics about how much time the average rep gets to spend in front of a customer. It's around 10 to 15 percent. That's not a lot of face time, but a lot of alone time. In sales, you need a lot of self-motivation and discipline. When things aren't going well, it's easy to get down and depressed. I've been there.

Many of the lessons I learned in athletics were helpful with this challenge. When playing any sport, there are a lot of failures. You get tired and knocked down, and sports help you learn that, as tiring as it might be, you must dig down and push through the physical pain and exhaustion. There are times when running one more lap seems impossible. Your legs feel like rubber, but somehow, you dig down and get it done. When participating in a team sport, your teammates can help pull you over the top. You see them overcoming things, so you feel like you can as well. You also feel obligated not to let your teammates down. Working alone as a rep, you must somehow summon that spirit to keep going. You must pull yourself up and keep going.

Many self-help books and methods are available to help you overcome motivation, boredom, rejection, and failure. Ultimately, different techniques work for different people. Regardless of their profession, staying upbeat and motivated is challenging for everyone. No matter what job you have, the routines can become boring, and it can be difficult to stay motivated. Certainly, in sales, we all have those times when we are lonely and down, and we need ways to overcome these feelings.

When I'm down, I know I need to take action of some type. The action can be physical or mental. I can make a few phone calls, send some emails, go for a walk, or go to the gym. I may allow myself a few minutes to wallow, and then I must take some action. Even if I'm faking it, being outwardly positive helps. Being around other people helps. A good attitude is helpful. I love the saying, "Make yourself a great day."

**When I'm down, I know I need to take action of some type.**

While at Rockport, I reported to the vice president of sales, who came to our company from Reebok. Rockport had been growing fast; however, there were major problems with inventory, pricing, and product assortment. Reebok had purchased Rockport, and this experienced manager came over to help fix these problems and continue to build sales.

Early in his tenure, we were at an industry show. For three mornings in a row, we both got on the elevator at the same time. Each morning, I said, "Good morning, Bob. How's it going?"

And each morning, he responded with a resounding, "Excellent!"

I knew we were heading to a conference with a lot of customers who had some significant problems—poor shipping, inconsistent product quality, and discounting of the product among them—and they'd be pounding on this manager all day. He was on his way to a full day of dealing with many issues and unhappy customers. Although he'd probably had the same type of day yesterday, he responded to my question with a positive, upbeat *Excellent!*

In the following months, in all my encounters with this man, he was always the same—upbeat and positive—but not in an overboard way. We had a lot of meetings, and after a quick, upbeat message, we'd get into the details. It struck me how consistent he was in the face of long, demanding days and issues.

I once worked with a colleague who came down with a very serious life-threatening ailment. The probability of full recovery was not good, and the months of chemo, surgery, and rehab were difficult. I'd worked with him before this ailment, and he was always upbeat and positive. When hit with this threat, he got even more positive. He never complained. He was convinced he would be in the small percentage of patients who defeated this disease, and he did—completely. I marveled at his attitude and do not doubt that his positive spirit contributed to his body defeating the disease. It's now many years later, and he's living a full life and is free of the disease. I see pictures of him with his grandkids and always remember how he handled a life-threatening disease and how his positive attitude was a major factor in his recovery.

I've had quite a few surgeries myself. Three back procedures, a hip replacement, a knee replacement that had to be done twice, and wrist surgery. I always said to myself, "I'm injured; I'm not sick," which is a big difference. My knee replacement had to be redone after one year. The surgeon had to remove the first replacement and put in a new one. The rehab for a knee is difficult and painful and takes several months. The physical therapist yanks and pulls on the knee to help reduce the scar tissue so that the knee can fully flex after rehab. Getting into the car to drive over to PT, I knew it would hurt like hell, but if I went with a good attitude, it really helped.

When the doctor told me a year later that I had to go through it again, I thought of my former colleague and how he would have handled it. For consecutive years from March through August, I lost being able to play golf and many other things I enjoyed. My days were all about rehab, getting through the most painful parts, and building up my knee via the exercises and weights. I always thought about how so many people were dealing with illnesses and injuries that were a whole lot worse than mine. If you want to count your blessings, walk into a rehab center or the waiting room of a pain management office. It keeps things in perspective when you see what other people are going through.

I'm a big believer in positive visualization. Positive visualization is a technique of imagination to envision the success you want to achieve. Some people meditate deeply and use all their senses to go through every aspect of the activity they want to achieve. If you have a major presentation or meeting, in your mind's eye, put on the clothes you'll wear that day, sit in the car, pretend to drive to the meeting, get out of the car and walk into the meeting and see the buyer, make the presentation, and receive the feedback and result you want. The rehearsal and practice build confidence, and while there will always be butterflies in your stomach, practicing helps relieve that nervousness. One of my favorite quotes is, "When it comes time to perform, everything leaves you except your

> **Positive visualization is a technique of imagination and practice to envision the success you want to achieve.**

practice." When I knew I'd prepared and practiced well, I could see my desired success and outcome. Of course, it's not just about the practice; you must also study and prepare and do all the work that the task calls for.

I believe in the combination of practice and positive visualization. Certainly, training your mind is a very powerful tool; however, I also need to know that I've practiced the desired outcome. A simple analogy for me is foul shooting in basketball. I often took at least 100 foul shots daily, and seeing that ball go into the net reinforced the positive outcome. In preparing for games, my confidence from having practiced the shot so many times and the mental image of seeing the ball go through the net built great confidence. In games when I was nervous, I could calm myself and simply go through the same physical routine I'd practiced. On two occasions, I went to the foul line for two shots, down one point and with no time on the clock. I am proud to say that I made both shots.

In preparing for selling situations, be it cold calling, presenting, or handling objections, I practiced and prepared mentally to envision successful outcomes. When I went into sales meetings, I always expected the outcome to be successful because I'd prepared well.

Having a positive mindset is contagious. In observing the reps I've worked with, the buyer also senses confidence or the lack of it. Remember that buyers work with many sales reps, and they know who's prepared and confident and who's not.

I heard a presentation from Nick Faldo, the great British golfer who won multiple major championships. He said, "Whenever a golfer goes into his bag on a par three over water for an old ball, he is on his way to hitting the ball in the water." He advises never to put a negative thought in your head; don't think about putting the ball in the water. Instead, think about seeing the ball landing on the green. Positive thoughts will lead to positive outcomes.

One year, I spoke to doctors in thirty-five cities, mostly in hotel ballrooms or breakout rooms. Whenever possible, the night before, I would go into the room and practice. I would feel the room's lights, smell the carpet, envision the audience, and practice the presentation. While on a plane, I often go into the bathroom (as small as they are) and close my eyes. I'd see myself walking up to the podium and looking around the room, and I would practice my presentation.

**Studying and preparing, and then practicing, can help overcome the fear of performance, which is what a sales call is.**

I went through the same routines before any important sales meeting. At home, I'd use our dining room table and pretend I was in a conference room. I'd go through all the parts of the call, including pretending to hand out folders, asking questions, and responding to expected objections and questions. Studying and preparing, and then practicing, can help overcome the fear of performance, which is what a sales call is.

Tips to stay motivated:

- Positive visualization
- Set short-term goals with rewards
- Take action
- Practice
- Take a break

Overcoming a lack of motivation is difficult. When I know I'm out of juice and need a jump start, I set a goal and reward myself. If I know I need to make a certain number of calls or secure a set number of orders, I get to do something I want to do when I achieve that goal. Sometimes, the best thing I can do is to take a break—sometimes for a couple of hours, sometimes for a couple of days—to recharge. I try to take off one weekend day, and I won't allow myself into my office on that day. We all need to get away from work. Creating balance in my life has been a factor when I've had motivation problems. I've also found that reaching out to some older relatives or friends who may need my support is a good way to leave my problems behind and help someone else.

## A WIN A DAY

When you know you're a bit down and need a boost, use whatever tactic works for you to recharge. That's a step in the right direction.

## WHAT I LEARNED IN COACHING THAT HELPED SECURE A WIN A DAY

I've experienced a lot of failure and rejection in both playing and coaching, which was a good training ground for my career in sales. It's hard to recover from poor performance by a team, and I questioned myself as a coach. What could I have done better to prepare the team? When we played well, I asked, *How can we keep this going?*

I ask myself these same questions following a sales call. What went well? What didn't, and how can I improve?

## FOR FURTHER THOUGHT:

- What are some ways you motivate yourself when your enthusiasm and motivation are low?
- How can you use positive visualization?

# 9

## THE ROAD WARRIOR LIFE

There's a song by Johnny Cash called "I've Been Every-where." Over the last forty years, I can relate to that song. I am a Million Miler on United Airlines and Titanium level at Bonvoy/Marriott. When I walk past gates at airports, I look at the destination of each flight, and at almost all of them, I say to myself, *I've been there.* I often come home after a trip and tell my wife, "We could live there." Sometimes, I come home and say, "Thank G-d we don't live there."

I've attended conferences and meetings at great resorts and hotels in almost every state. Orlando and Las Vegas made wise decisions to build gigantic convention centers that can host meetings of all sizes. Some hotels do a great job hosting meetings, and others don't. I recently attended a meeting in a renovated bank of all places. It turned out to be a great venue; our group was the only one in the facility, and the staff was super attentive because all they did was host meetings. Before the meeting, all vendors were directed to send their conference materials to a FedEx store right across the street, which was convenient.

But there was a problem. It just so happened that on the day of the conference, a sizable parade was scheduled to march on the main street where the bank and FedEx office were located. Because of that, FedEx decided to close the store that day. To compound the issue, many vendors had scheduled their delivery for the morning of the conference. When FedEx's delivery trucks arrived at the closed store, the shipments were returned to the FedEx warehouse. None of the vendors could get their boxes and materials for the conference.

Stuff just happens, and it's often nobody's fault. My rule of thumb is always to arrive a day early, so when I checked on our materials and realized we wouldn't be able to get our shipments, my colleague and I went to the FedEx warehouse to pick up our materials. It took some special assistance from FedEx to locate our boxes within their facility, but they were helpful.

**My rule of thumb is always to arrive a day early . . .**

It gets frustrating and disappointing when I've been to a city and have seen only the airport and hotel. My favorite business travel is when I've been able to drive around an area, see the local spots, and meet people. People are pretty much the same wherever you go, and I enjoy learning about the places I am. One of my favorite cities is Chicago. While it's a big city, the people are just as friendly as in small towns, and the restaurants are all great (although I'm not a deep-dish pizza fan). I also love Atlanta. I went to the University of Georgia, which is sixty-five miles northeast of Atlanta, and the southern charm and hospitality are always reminders of my college days.

I've been going to Phoenix for over forty years. My college roommate, Mark Curtis, has been the sports and news anchor there all these years, and when he first arrived, I worked at the Arizona State Basketball Camp. Converse and Rockport held their national meetings there, and my family has vacationed

75

there many times. One of our favorite things is tube down the Snake River in Mesa. When it's 100 degrees outside, we sit in tubes in the cool water and paddle down to see horses drinking from the stream and hawks flying overhead. One cautionary tale: Never leave your prescription glasses in the car when it's 100 degrees. I did, and when we got back to the car after a few hours on the river, my glasses were melted.

I also like the Northwest, Vancouver, and Seattle in particular. In Vancouver, you see many people from diverse backgrounds, and the air feels fresher and cleaner.

It takes some time to learn how to travel efficiently and effectively. You need to have discipline while on the road, and it helps to be flexible because there are frequent delays and hurdles. I am a type-A when it comes to travel. I know I'm more productive and relaxed if I know where I'm going and when I'll be there. So, I plan every aspect of a trip. Now with Google and other online programs, it's much easier.

I was fortunate to be a graduate assistant basketball coach at the University of Georgia. While most graduate assistant coaches do a lot of minor tasks, my role became much larger because the two full-time assistant coaches said they wouldn't leave the state of Georgia to recruit. I was responsible for recruiting the rest of the country. This was an incredible opportunity at a very young age. I was given a national airline credit card and told to hit the road and find some players. Being from New York City, that's where I went most often. I still had a lot of friends and contacts, and I regularly traveled to New York and the Tri-State area to find players. I learned at this young age how to travel and get around.

Keep in mind that this was 1978: pre-internet, no Google Maps, no cell phones. Before I left home, I often called the police department for directions because I knew they'd know the area and could give me some tips about how to get around. This was helpful in later years when I started traveling to towns

I'd never been to before. Sometimes when I spoke with the police and gave them the address, they'd say, "That's a shoe store," and I would say, "Yes, that's where I need to go." They weren't all that pleased because they probably thought I'd wanted to go to a little more significant place like a hospital or court building.

There are always hurdles and problems that arise when traveling for work. A plane can get delayed or canceled. There can be traffic accidents or just traffic congestion. Your luggage can be lost. It's easy to be pulled away and distracted when traveling for work.

**There are always hurdles and problems that arise when traveling for work.**

There are also the personal challenges of being away from home. It's lonely and can be depressing. You miss some important events at home. It's also challenging if you must work with someone you don't like or someone loud or inconsiderate. It's also physically tiring. You either must drive or fly, often after long days.

When I sold for Aetrex and scanning technology, I flew into Minneapolis to meet with the two largest golf retailers in the country, Golf Galaxy and Golfsmith. It just so happened that both headquarters were in the same city, and after many months of calling and tracking down the buyers, I got appointments with each of them on consecutive days. It's hard enough to get an appointment with one buyer, let alone two.

Our company had a new foot scanner they could place in their stores to scan customers for Callaway inserts. The scanner was sent via UPS to my hotel. This was an early version of a scanner about the size of a standard card table. It weighed about thirty pounds and had a good number of moving parts. When I got to my hotel and asked if there was a delivery for me, I was told nothing had arrived. That was the start of my cold sweating for the next few hours.

The hotel was in an office park setting, and two other hotels were very close together. I went over to hotel number two, and again, no box. Finally, I saw the box at the third hotel, stacked behind the front desk. When I picked it up, my heart sank, and I was nauseous in less than five seconds. When I picked up the box, I could hear a lot of parts rattling around.

I quickly checked in, went to my room, and called our tech person to tell him what was happening. He told me to unbox the scanner, turn it over, and unscrew the seventeen screws that kept the two parts of the scanner in place. I went down to the front desk, and miraculously they had a screwdriver. (From then on, I always traveled with one.) I returned to my room, and the tech guy talked me through the inner workings of the scanner. Several parts had come loose, and after about an hour, somehow, someway, it worked. My presentations were the next day. The lesson is to be like a good Boy Scout—always be prepared and expect the unexpected.

One of my most surprising travel experiences was on Cape Cod in Massachusetts. I was staying at a Holiday Inn. At about 10:00 p.m., there was an explosion. It sounded like something had been thrown through a window, like a garbage can. Shortly after, there was another similar sound and a loud siren, and it felt like the walls were shaking. I called the front desk and asked what in the world was going on.

The front desk person said, "Well, all that commotion is from the state police staying here, and they're getting kind of rowdy. Not much we can do to quiet down the state police."

For the next few hours, there were periods of quiet and then some more beer cans being thrown around and other horseplay. I didn't get much sleep that night, and when I checked out the next morning, there was no charge for the room.

After all these years on the road, I thought I'd share some of my top travel tips. Anytime I meet a fellow road warrior, I always ask what tips they have. That's how we all learn from each other.

**My top travel tips:**

- Always get a room with two beds. Put everything on the second bed except your hanging blazer, pants, etc. Do not put anything in any drawer. This way, you always know where everything is.
- If I'm traveling with my wife and have only one bed, I use the ironing board for storing all my clothes and items.
- Disconnect the clock by the bed. Don't waste time trying to figure out if the alarm is set or not. I've had too many alarms go off much earlier than I wanted to wake.
- When packing, roll all your items. This saves space and prevents wrinkles. Stuff socks and anything else you can inside shoes. You can store a lot in there. I'm a size thirteen, so I can stuff in quite a bit.
- Pack as you unpack. When you return from a trip, replace everything you take from your travel bag so you're already packed for the next trip.
- Have duplicates of everything you travel with. Don't take anything from your home office. Have a travel set of everything you need for work at the hotel or on the plane: chargers, external battery pack, etc. Same for your toiletry bag. Have a second bag with everything you need to travel with.
- Call the hotel a few hours before you arrive. Confirm that your room will be ready by the time you get there. Ask for the person's name that you speak with.
- Check how the gas tank opens before you leave the rental car facility. Some can be tricky to find. I once had to drive to a dealership because I couldn't figure out how to open the gas tank.
- For special trips, call the hotel GM and ask him/her for an upgrade if available.

- Use the clips on the hangers to fully close the curtains in the hotel room. They never match up completely, and this will provide you with a dark room for sleep.
- Tip everyone: bellman, room maids, rental car drivers, van drivers if you park off site. These people are not well paid, and they can be helpful.
- Ask the locals where to go. At conferences, I ask the waiters or other local staff where to eat, the best way to get around, etc. These people live in the area and know where to go for almost everything.
- Get some form of exercise. Hit the workout room or go for a walk, early or late, whichever you prefer.
- Don't eat in your room. Go out. It refreshes you, and the room won't smell like pizza or whatever you bring. If you must bring in food, eat in the lobby. (This is just my preference.)
- Always leave thirty minutes earlier than you think you should.
- If possible, do something other than stay in the room. Go to a movie, a ballgame, a mall. Be where there are people.
- For plane or railroad trips, always have an extra book, some work, or a long-term project for those long, unexpected delays. I've sat on runways and been told we were number twenty-two for takeoff, which could mean an hour or more of idle time.
- Keep an extra bag in your travel bag in case you bring home some things you didn't have at the start of your trip.
- Keep an envelope in your briefcase or backpack and put all your receipts there. On the outside, record any expense notes. I know most people enter this info into their phones, and there are efficient apps for this. I also like to have the receipts organized in one place, the envelope.

- Keep some key medicines in a baggie in your briefcase, like Tums, Advil, Alegra, etc.
- FlightAware is a great app that tells you where a plane is coming from, the expected arrival time, and the gate number.
- When you leave the room to check out, walk out of the room with all your bags and then go back in for one quick look around. My buddy Kevin McNally gave me that tip, and I always think of him when I re-enter the room and check.

## A WIN A DAY

Consider it a win when you're on time, prepared, and stress free or when a curve ball comes at you, and you handle it.

## WHAT I LEARNED IN COACHING THAT HELPED SECURE A WIN A DAY

While traveling as a coach, I was responsible for players and staff, which is a bit more complicated than traveling alone. I learned that you can't please everybody. If I took a team for dinner, some players might like the place, and others won't. I made the best decision I could for the group as a whole and hoped for the best.

The most crucial element of travel is always to do your best to plan for all aspects and contingencies.

## FOR FURTHER THOUGHT:

- What are some of your tips for traveling effectively?

# 10

## MY MENTORS AND WHAT I LEARNED FROM THEM

I feel so fortunate to have had several mentors in my life in addition to the love and support of my parents. Many times in my personal and professional life, I needed some advice and someone to talk to. I'd like to tell you about some of my most significant mentors and how they helped me. I'm grateful to each of them and a few others not included on this list.

### DICK LOYND

Dick was Group Vice President of Allied Chemical and spearheaded the move for Allied to purchase Converse. At the time, Allied had over 100 brand products, but none were direct to the consumer except for Converse, which became a problem. As a rep, I was part of a region with twenty-five reps, and the decision was made to split the region. I became the regional manager for this new unit.

Dick had opened an office in New Jersey, where he and I lived, so I shared an office with him. The Converse headquarters was in Massachusetts. My exposure to Dick became a bit of an issue for the senior managers at Converse. They were concerned about how I'd interact with Dick and what I could say that they might not want him to know. I understood this touchy issue, and over time, I handled it well. I never had any problem with the senior managers at Converse regarding my discussions with Dick.

We often had lunch together if we were both in the office on the same day. Spending time with him was like getting an MBA. He lettered in four sports at Cornell at age sixteen. At one point in his career, he worked in Minneapolis while his family lived in New Jersey. He left every Sunday and returned on Friday nights—for several years.

One time, I observed that he had a very busy few days of flying to multiple cities with full schedules of meetings and dinners, etc. I asked him how he could keep up with it all.

"Stu," he said. "You need a big engine."

Dick was tough, demanding, and intimidating. He wrote about gross profit management and elevated many of the practices at Converse. He instituted monthly performance reviews, which were a full day of round-table presentations from every manager in the company. It was a grind, and you had to be prepared and on top of all areas of your responsibilities. Several very competent and experienced people were nervous during these sessions. I attended these meetings when I was promoted to director of national accounts. I saw these meetings as an opportunity to show that you were doing your job.

Dick said, "Always be truthful when reporting. Give us the good, the bad, and everything in between. We must truly know what's going on in every area of the business."

What I learned most from Mr. Loynd was simply tell the truth on all issues. There's no need to sugarcoat anything.

Senior management needs to know what's really going on. I also learned to have a plan to make progress or fix a problem.

## SHELLY SCHNEIDER

Shelly was the head boys' basketball coach of Brooklyn Tech High School in Brooklyn, NY. Brooklyn Tech is one of two New York City high schools that required an entrance exam for admission. The other was Stuyvesant High School, and a student had to have the academic credentials to attend either school.

What was a bit frustrating for Shelley was that Brooklyn Tech was in the Fort Green section of Brooklyn, and a staggering number of some of New York City's best basketball players grew up very close to the school. But none attended Tech because of the entrance exam and the required academic credentials.

However, Shelley did get a good number of outstanding players. Charlie Davis became an All-American at Wake Forest and played for many years in the NBA. Ronnie Nunn was also a great player who attended George Washington University and played professionally in Mexico. After playing, he became an NBA official.

During the summers, Shelly ran the waiter program at Tyler Hill Camp in Pennsylvania. In most camps, the waiters were relegated to inferior accommodations and separated from the camp, usually without access to the camp's facilities. Shelly had a different vision for a waiter program. He created a full, competitive athletic program for the waiters where they played games after every meal in all sports. He recruited several outstanding basketball players to work as waiters, and they played games against the other camps in the area. Shelly worked at the camp for twenty-five years, and the team never lost a game.

I was fortunate to meet up with Shelly through some coaches he knew, and he brought me to the camp. After years as a waiter and counselor, I joined him as his assistant in running the waiter program. I learned much from him about leadership and managing people, particularly young people. I learned how to give firm, clear directions and how to take charge of a large group. We met as a group before every meal and outlined what the marching orders were.

The waiter program had forty fifteen- and sixteen-year-olds. Shelly told me, "If we're not organized and in control, these kids could wreck the place."

I also learned to try to make as many tasks as fun as possible. As waiters, we had to do some mundane tasks throughout the week since we had a workforce of forty young bodies to throw at any project. No matter the task, Shelly always designed a way to make it fun and upbeat. He set the tone, and once there was discipline and clear direction, we could have fun and a lot of laughs.

Above all else, what I learned from Shelly was how to help and mentor young people. He was always available to listen to and help all of these young people in those uncomfortable teenage years who had a lot of issues to deal with. I know because I was one of those kids; his support and guidance helped me deal with those struggles. He is someone who, if you ask him, will tell you exactly how he feels about the question. You may not like the response, but you know that his answer is honest. So many other people might hedge or not tell you what they're thinking, and it's a great comfort to receive a truthful perspective from someone you admire and respect.

Shelly has been in my life for over fifty years. We speak at least once a week, and after all these years, I don't think we've ever had a conversation where we don't laugh a lot. I still learn from him and am so fortunate to have had his guidance and support all these years.

## JOHN BUNYAN

Mr. Bunyan was my high school basketball coach. I write "Mr. Bunyan," and let me tell you why. I stayed in touch with him for fifty years until his passing. I was honored to speak at his eighty-fifth birthday celebration and funeral. We started every phone conversation the same way.

I would call and say, "Hi, Mr. Bunyan. It's Stu."

He would say, "Stuie, please call me John," but I just couldn't do it. He was a major influence in my life, and I had too much respect for him to ever call him by his first name.

He'd been in the Army and came to teaching and coaching after his service. There were very few black head basketball coaches in New York City when he got the job. I'm sure he dealt with many racial injustices in the service and the mostly white New York City coaching circles. Mr. Bunyan was a drill-sergeant type in the gym and in running the basketball program. There were no shortcuts.

What I appreciated and learned most from him was his preparation. He went to see all our opponents play and came back to practice with a plan for what we would face, particularly the press defenses and offensive alignments of these teams. I was the point guard on our team and had to handle the full-court and half-court defenses. He and I had a lot of conversations regarding my responsibilities. His scouting and planning stayed with me, and I ran many of the same practice drills and game sets I learned from him when I got into coaching.

We were a challenging group. While he never lost his composure, there were times when he was frustrated about how we were playing, and he let us know it. He was demanding but never demeaning.

We were expected to be a very good team my senior year. We didn't start the season too well; however, he kept us on track. We got on a roll and eventually won the borough of Brooklyn and made it to New York City's Final Four played at Madison Square Garden.

When I got the head coaching position at Pace University, I called him and asked him to be my assistant coach. He thought about it briefly and politely declined. We stayed in touch until his final days. I can still hear his resounding voice in my mind calling out to us during practices and games. He ended all our phone calls with the same advice.

He would say, "Stuie, enjoy, enjoy, enjoy."

## GENE WESTMORELAND

Gene was the athletic director of Pace University. He was also the head baseball and basketball coach. He spent fourteen years at Pace, and, as the school grew from a college to a university, he played a huge role in building the athletic department. He was an outstanding athlete. He played on the Pace baseball, basketball, golf, and track teams. Gene is in the Pace University Hall of Fame, and the baseball dugout is named after him with a magnificent plaque with his likeness and accomplishments listed. An honor well deserved for all his contributions to the university.

After Pace, Gene moved to an executive position at the Metropolitan Golf Association. Met Golf is the sanctioning organization for hundreds of courses and tournaments in the Tri-State region. Gene became an internationally renowned expert on the rules of golf. He's been an active member of the United States Golf Association and has served as co-chairman of the US Amateur and US Open championships. He's written for several golf publications and is the author of *A Game for Life: Golf's Rules and Rewards*.

I played for Gene at Pace and stayed in touch with him when I transferred to Georgia. I served as his assistant basketball coach and succeeded him as head coach. Gene was juggling the administrative tasks of being the athletic director and coaching two sports. He was always under control and a gentleman in how he treated everyone. I don't ever remember him ever losing his composure.

I was a young head coach at twenty-three years old. I remember my first scrimmage against another college, and Gene came to watch. We played terribly. We were completely outplayed and outcoached, and I was disappointed and embarrassed.

"It looks like we've never even practiced together," I said. "We could barely execute anything we've worked on."

"Stu," he said. "In coaching, on bad days, you're never as bad as you think you look, and on good days, you're never as good as you think you look. So, keep things in perspective."

I've remembered that advice many times over the years.

Currently, Gene is an active member at Wing Foot Golf Club in Westchester, one of the most historic and respected courses in all of golf. He serves on several committees, which is typical of him in that he always contributes to any organization or group he's a part of. I've continued to stay in regular touch with Gene and appreciate his advice and friendship.

## HERB KUTZEN

Herb was ahead of his time in many ways. He and his wife Melanie were both teachers. When they decided to purchase Bryne Mawr Camp in Honesdale, Pennsylvania, Herb left teaching and became the first full-time camp owner. He and Melanie built Bryne Mawr into one of the top girl's camps in the country. Following the summer sessions, Bryne Mawr was also the site of the famous Five Star Basketball Camp, so Herb created an extended season for the use of the camp.

Herb was also ahead of his time because he was a basketball coach and built programs like today's AAU organizations.

He ran the basketball programs for the Jewish Community House, the Flatbush Jewish Center, and the East Flatbush Ruby YMCA. I played for him in the years before high school, and I learned the game from him. We played many games all over New York City. Herb kept a lot of statistics well beyond the usual basics of shots taken and made, rebounds and assists, foul shots, etc. He had some formulas that measured your effectiveness while on the court, combining all the different statistics. While these analytics are used in all sports today, back when Herb created them, they weren't commonly a part of many programs and certainly not in youth basketball.

Herb allowed me to play on teams of players a few years older than me, which helped my skills and development. Herb was very direct in his analysis and coaching methods. Many times, he told me how I needed to improve. I remember some post-game conversations that were direct and certainly got my attention.

After one game where I hadn't had a very good shooting percentage, he asked me, "Did it ever occur to you to stop taking jump shots? Did it occur to you when you kept missing to maybe think about driving to the basket to get fouled? If you're going to keep taking jump shots, did it occur to you to maybe try a bank shot now and then?" None of those things *had* occurred to me, but from then on, they did.

Herb was also part of a significant development in my playing career. As a ninth grader at Ditmas Junior High School, I probably had the best single season in my playing career. We won the borough of Brooklyn. In the spring of that year, I went to the high school for workouts and tryouts in front of the high school coach. I played well and was going to be on the varsity team for my sophomore year.

During that summer, I worked at a camp that Herb ran, and we played games all over the Pennsylvania mountains. At the end of the summer, Herb advised me not to play on the high school team. He thought I wouldn't get much playing time, so I wouldn't improve. He suggested I play on his team, where we'd play sixty games, and I would get better.

So, in the fall when school started, I didn't show up for the basketball team workouts. The coach called me into his office and asked why I hadn't shown up, and I told him that rather than not getting much playing time on the varsity team, I was going to play for Herb and get a lot more minutes on the court and hope to improve. Other advisers told me that if I didn't pay my dues, sit on the bench, and learn as a sophomore, I probably wouldn't be allowed back on the team. I played for Herb and got stronger and better. Fortunately, Mr. Bunyan allowed me back on the team as a junior, and I wound up starting. Herb was one of the most influential mentors in my teenage years, and I'm grateful for all the time, energy, and advice he gave me.

## JOHN GUTHRIE

John was Head Coach of the University of Georgia. Shelly Schneider connected me to him, and I transferred to Georgia after playing one year at Pace. When someone writes a book about the best recruiters in college basketball, there should be a chapter about John. He recruited several high school All Americans and out-recruited many of the nation's top programs. He was relentless in his pursuit of the players he wanted, outworking many other coaches. He was an excellent judge of talent, and a friendly southern gentleman, whose smile and laughter lit up the room. People were drawn to his fun-loving personality and easy-going manner.

John arranged for me to be an assistant coach at Clarke Central High School in Athens, Georgia, during my senior year, and then he brought me onto his staff the following year. I was with him and the team 24/7, and he gave me plenty of responsibilities, particularly in recruiting. He sent me all over Georgia and many other areas to evaluate players. At a very young age, I was exposed to the highest level of Division I college basketball, including player development, scouting opponents, practice preparation, and the administrative tasks of coaching a college program. I always thought of John's friendly and fun spirit and tried to emulate his personality with my players.

When I was coaching, I always tried to connect in some way with every player at the start of the day with either a brief tap on the shoulder or high five and then ask him how he was doing. I stayed in contact with John for forty years after working with him. We had some great times playing golf and having dinners; he became one of my best friends. I checked in with him on every significant development in my life.

## DR. MARC BRENNER

Marc is truly one of the world's leading experts in diabetic foot care management and wound care. Patients from all over the world travel to his office for his evaluation and treatment. He is tireless in his efforts to heal every patient who comes to him. He's a past president of The American Society of Podiatric Dermatology. Marc has been an advisor and lecturer for a long list of global medical companies, and he's taught hundreds of doctors how to provide better care for their patients.

Marc was a top major league baseball prospect coming out of college, and he played in the Yankees organization before attending medical school. To this day, the Yankees continue sending their players with foot and ankle injuries to him for evaluation.

Marc is my go-to guru for learning about anything related to the foot and how to best present any information to the medical profession. Marc has been my career advisor. He never hesitates to tell me exactly how he feels about any issue I bring up. I know he'll always give me his honest opinion, which is greatly appreciated.

## FOR FURTHER THOUGHT:

Name a mentor you have and tell what you have learned from him or her.

# 11

# THE ABSOLUTE BEST OF THE BEST

## STEVE FREEMAN

Steve is by far the best rep I've ever been around. I believe he grew up in the shoe business because his product and industry knowledge were outstanding. He always knew every aspect of the customer's business, their needs, and how the product could benefit them, providing the features and benefits, costs, margins, etc. Steve had the New York City territory, with some tough and demanding retailers. All of them greatly respected him because they could count on him for his professionalism and support of their business.

I managed Steve at Rockport. When I needed information about weekly activity and other aspects of the business, no matter what I asked for, Steve always had his information and reports in ahead of everyone else. I asked him why he always turned things around so quickly, and he said, "I realized that it took longer to wallow, complain, and procrastinate than it did to just answer the questions or do the report."

After Rockport, Steve moved on to a high-end women's brand from France, where he helped design and sell the product. Steve made the best presentations I've ever observed. He had an easy flow to his cadence and product descriptions and always presented groups of products, never items. The full assortment, or at least several offerings, had to be purchased. He never allowed a retailer to cherry pick an item or two. He knew what would show and work best, and that's what he sold.

## BILL ADAMS

Bill became a teacher and baseball coach after his professional baseball days as a catcher in the Giants' organization. He later transitioned to a different career. He took a course on how to make a career change. That's a great example of how Bill worked. He was always well organized and had a plan for everything he undertook. Bill was a rep in the region I managed at Converse, and he succeeded me, first as a regional manager and then as the director of national accounts. I learned from Bill how to build relationships with accounts and be organized for all aspects of preparing for presentations.

Bill left Converse and moved to the New Era Hat Company, where he rose to be the general manager of North America and directed all the sales reps. He also became the point person to build New Era shops in stadiums throughout major league baseball. Bill is a valued advisor to many baseball team owners. During his tenure, New Era grew by hundreds of millions of dollars.

One of my fondest memories was spending a day on the road with Bill, visiting his accounts all day. We ended our day at his house, and as we walked in, we could hear both of his young children in the bathtub. Without missing a beat, he put down his briefcase, rolled up his sleeves, and knelt by the tub to finish their baths. I had no doubt where his priorities were. I learned from him how to best prepare and be organized, and he was also a role model for me as a dad.

## RONNIE NUNN

Ronnie grew up in Brooklyn and played at Brooklyn Tech High School. As a senior, he was a New York Post Top 10 All New York City selection. He then went on to George Washington University, where he scored 1,068 points. In 1997, he was inducted into GW's Hall of Fame. Following graduation, he played professionally in Mexico.

In 1984, he began his career as an NBA official, and for nineteen years, he officiated 1,173 regular season games, seventy-six playoff games, and four NBA Finals. He then served as the director of NBA officials for five years.

Before joining the NBA, Ronnie was my assistant coach at Pace University. I learned a great deal from Ron in two areas: his game knowledge and his teaching and presentation skills. On the basketball side of things, he taught the Kentucky two-man drills, which helped players in all phases of their skills. This series became the foundation of the practices we incorporated at Pace. Ron also encouraged me to be more demanding with the players.

Ron is a dynamic public speaker, one of the best I've ever heard. He can captivate and control an audience via his powerful voice, timing, enthusiasm, and confidence. I modeled my on-court speaking style after Ron's, and when I found myself speaking at national and regional conferences, I emulated his powerful and effective delivery style.

## JASON KRAUS

I've worked for and with Jason for twenty-five years in the medical device and podiatry space. He founded Benefoot Labs and then became COO of Orthotic Holdings, Inc. He recently started Orthotica Labs. I mentioned Jason earlier in the book when I wrote about his philosophy of trusting the people he hired. He throws whatever comes his way over his shoulder, confident that the people behind him will catch it and do their jobs. He trusts the people he works with. There are no head games or politics, and there's always full transparency. Jason shares everything he knows on every subject and keeps everyone in the company informed about everything that's going on. His team-oriented attitude is always about *How can I help you?* There's no blame game. When issues or problems arise, it's all about *How can we fix this? How can I help? What do we need?*

I've never seen him lose his composure in all my years with Jason, in all the meetings, all the doctor and staff encounters, and all the conferences. Jason is a tireless worker. He's always the smartest person in the room but never calls attention to himself. I cannot say that I've been able to emulate all I've observed and learned from Jason, but I've had a great role model in him. He's head and shoulders the best business executive I've been around.

## CHRIS GACOS

Chris is the best retailer I've ever known. He and his brother Peter founded Sneakers Plus in Flemington, New Jersey, and over the last forty-five years, I've seen his athletic footwear and apparel business grow and prosper. This is a competitive category, and Chris had to adapt to the big box stores coming into his trading area and major brands' company-direct stores. Chris built long-term relationships with all the athletic directors and coaches in the schools that he works with. He's a visionary, and as the Internet was emerging, he started an online business, SP Custom Gear, to provide custom apparel and products for school teams, clubs, and businesses, which has grown to be a major business. Chris's wife, Fran, and his son, Christopher, are also key contributors to the business.

I've seen first-hand how attentive to customer service Chris and his team are, always going above and beyond to ensure everything is provided on time and to the customer's exact needs. Sneakers Plus and SP Custom Gear have built a world-class reputation, and I learn from Chris every time we are together.

## STEVEN SREBNICK

Steven is the hardest-working person in any field I've ever known. His work ethic is second to none. He was a rep at Converse, Rockport, Clarks, and Aetrex, exceeding his quota every season without fail. No matter what it took, he always found a way to write the number of orders he'd set as a goal. I was his manager at these companies, except during his time at Clarks. I remember leaving a meeting where he'd received a sizable order, and when I congratulated him, he wasn't satisfied because they hadn't ordered one style.

When I traveled with Steven, there were many days when I was ready to finish the day, but he always had a few more stops to make. He raised my performance level on the days I traveled with him. There's no way that I ever matched his work ethic.

In 2018, he purchased an established shoe store in Rehoboth Beach, Delaware, called Fit 2 Soles. I thought this was a perfect career move for him because I knew that owning a shoe store is truly a 24/7 undertaking, and if there was anyone I'd choose to own a shoe store, it would be Steven—because of his work ethic. The store is a major success, achieving weekly, monthly, and seasonal year-over-year growth well beyond industry standards.

A recent magazine poll of consumers in Delaware voted Fit 2 Soles as the best shoe store in the region. Even when many consumers purchase via the Internet, his retail store thrives. The consumer has responded to all the brands and services Steven and his staff provide. The days are long and hard, and Steven grinds and grinds, works, and succeeds, which he well deserves.

## BARRY NEUBERGER

Barry and I worked and lived together when he started his career as a college administrator at Pace. He then moved on to positions at NYU, DePaul, Georgia State, Oakland University, Columbia, and Yeshiva University. Barry is not included in this list because we've been best friends for forty-five years. He's on my list of the best because of what I've learned from him, all that he's accomplished, and how he goes about his business.

Do you know someone absolutely everyone admires and likes, someone no one's ever said a negative word about? Barry is that person. I've spent time with him at every school where he's worked, and he is universally liked and admired.

His key strength has been marketing the various colleges within the communities. We often went to dinner in these university towns, and Barry was greeted like the mayor. In most cases, we couldn't get a bill for the meal we'd enjoyed. These were the owners of businesses that he sold to, and they treated him so well.

Barry gets along with everyone: coworkers, coaches, players, and anyone he's ever worked with and for. College presidents, coaches, business owners, doormen—everybody likes him. He's easy to talk to, a great listener, smart, and fun, and he's been my best friend for many years. I'm so grateful for his friendship.

## DR. ANDREAS ROTSIDES

There are still a few special old-school doctors who follow up when you call, care about you, and even make house calls. Dr. Rotsides is this type of doctor. While he takes great care of me because we've been great friends for over thirty years, I know he treats all his patients with the same dedication and professionalism. Many times when we're together on the golf course or out for the night, when his phone rings, he takes the call. He ends just about every call with the same statement, "I'll take care of it." Often, he gets back on the phone with the pharmacy to order a prescription, contact the hospital, or order an exam—whatever it takes to help the patient. Andy's been honored by several groups for his patient care. Don't take my word for it. Here are a couple of reviews on RateMDs.

- Dr. Rotsides is a one-of-a-kind physician to us. Not only does he care deeply about our health, but he's also our trusted friend. I asked him once, "How do you remember so much about me?" He paused and said, "Because I listen and care."
- Dr. Rotside is a great doctor. Marvelous diagnostician, compassionate and friendly. I could go on and on.
- Wonderful Doctor, very approachable. Answers everything.
- Dr. Rotsides is a great doctor, very kind and understanding. I'm so grateful for his care and friendship.

## THE BEST OF THE BEST

Now, for the #1 Best of the Best. My wife, Helene, isn't on this list because of how wonderful she's been as a daughter, sister, wife, mother, and grandmother. She's on this list because of her forty-plus years as a registered nurse and coordinator in the operating room at Morristown Medical Center. Over all these years, I've been at hospital ceremonies, weddings, and parties and met many doctors, nurses, and administrators. When they learn that I'm Helene's husband, they go to great lengths to tell me how competent and dedicated she is and how much they admire her work ethic and professionalism. Several have told me that she has the hardest job in the hospital. She manages this complicated and high-stress position as a coordinator in the OR for a trauma one, thirty-room operating room department. Surgeons can be quite demanding and difficult to rein in, and they sometimes need to be appeased—and other times put in their place—all while ensuring the priority of outstanding patient care is met.

I've often seen Helene studying the next day's schedule and planning how to best coordinate all that has to fall in place the next day: which doctors work best with which nurses and which doctors are slow and require a backup plan for surgeries scheduled in the same room. It's a balancing act to pull it all together, and she does it well. Helene retired for just a few months before COVID hit, and when it did, she went back to the hospital to give ninety to a hundred vaccine shots a day. These were long and tiring days, and our whole family is proud of our family's Healthcare Hero.

## FOR FURTHER THOUGHT:

Who are some of the best people you've known, and what made them so effective?

# 12

---

## TOP QUOTES THAT INSPIRE ME

Quotes have always inspired me. I keep a list of them in a folder, and when I need some inspiration, I read them again. Below, I've included some of my favorite quotes with my thoughts on each.

**"Never put off to tomorrow what you can do today."**
**~ Benjamin Franklin**

This advice has helped me many times throughout my career. While some projects need a good deal of time to complete, there are many projects and tasks that can and should be done when they arise.

I start each day with a to-do list, and my goal is to complete everything on that list. Each day is usually busy, and finishing each day's workload gives you a sense of accomplishment and satisfaction. And when you take the time to complete a project before it's due, when you aren't rushing or under a close deadline, you have the luxury of returning to it to take another look and edit it. My first pass at an assignment isn't usually my best work, and I may have some additional information or thoughts that come to mind. Creating the foundation today gives me a baseline for when I need to submit the work. And if I can finish today's work, other larger and more demanding projects often arrive the following day. If I didn't finish yesterday's work, I now have a lot more to do in less time.

**"Do unto others as you would have others do unto you."**
**~ Matthew 7:12**

I tell everyone I've ever hired or coached that I only have one rule for everyone, and it's this: I want to treat everyone I work with the same way I would want to be treated, and I expect the same in return. It's a simple and well-understood concept by people of all ages, making so much sense.

In coaching, there are many ways to make a point without embarrassing a player. Same with working with sales reps and customers. In many ways, I've never stopped being a sales rep. As a manager, you do a lot of selling, and as a manager, I've always reported to senior management. I know how challenging the sales job is. Some managers may have sold in the past and quickly forget how it feels when you're out on your own, responsible for bringing in the business.

There's a fair and professional way to discuss anything with anyone who reports to you. There's never a reason to be curt, short, or disrespectful. I always think about what it feels like to be on the other side of the conversation.

This same philosophy applies to delivering good news, compliments, and constructive criticism. We all can use a pat on the back and congratulations when there's a step in the right direction. Providing positive feedback is just as important—or maybe more so—than providing constructive, negative feedback. I search for ways to deliver compliments and good news on whatever level of accomplishment. Make people feel good about themselves.

I don't like to be micromanaged, and I don't know anyone who does. There are many positive reasons and results to give your people the freedom to make their own decisions. I believe that most people want to do a good job and are invested in their area of responsibility. In most cases, the person knows much more about the overall picture than the person who micromanages them. It takes so much energy to update a micromanager and to negotiate with this person on their suggested input.

Jason Kraus, one of the very best owners/managers I have ever worked for, told me several times that he trusts the people he hired. He throws whatever comes his way over his shoulder, believing that the people responsible for whatever had been presented will catch the project and do their jobs. I feel the same way. Let people do their jobs, give them all the help and information they need, and treat them as you want to be treated. When you treat people how you want to be treated, they provide much more because they're invested and feel responsible for the outcome. I don't think the people I manage work for me; in fact, I believe I work for them. Often, a rep will introduce me as their boss, and I always tell the customer, "No, I work for Sarah. She's the boss."

Often managers parachute into a territory to see a customer for various reasons. The visit could be to introduce new programs, or it could be because there are problems. On many occasions, the people I've managed have gone out of their way to make sure I wasn't blindsided, unprepared, or embarrassed in any way. They've often given me a heads-up on how to best handle a potential issue, especially if there's a problem, and they've prepared solutions. This creates a trust factor in the relationship and a strong bond of working together. I am very proud of these relationships; they're built on deep mutual respect and friendship.

### "It's easier to ask forgiveness than to get permission."
#### ~ Rear Admiral Grace Hopper

I was managing a start-up program where we placed technology in doctor's offices nationwide. We sent in large screen TVs. As we rolled out the program, many of the TVs were damaged in shipping, and when they arrived, they were inoperable. My phone was ringing off the hook from our staff as they set up the systems. They weren't the only ones disappointed; the doctors were, too.

I got a call from one of our newest and youngest tech reps, and before I answered, I anticipated why he was calling—another rep who wanted to know what to do.

But he surprised me. He said, "Hi, Stu. I just wanted to let you know that the big screen TV was damaged when I showed up at the doctor's office, so I went to Best Buy and purchased a new one and set that up."

This is a great example on many levels. When I hung up the phone, I said to myself, *This young fellow will be very successful. Rather than asking for directions or permission or complaining, he took care of the problem and solved it.* Most of the rest of the staff were calling in to ask what to do.

Other people I've worked with also step forward and solve problems. These folks have been some of my favorite people to work with, not because it saved me from solving the problem for them but because it showed how committed they were to getting the job done.

I've tried to adhere to this philosophy in my work when possible. I've always tried to be a problem solver, get the job done, and then report what I've done. In most cases, this has been well received by the people I've reported to.

## "You pass the same people on the way up as you do on the way down." ~ Walter Winchell

I can hear my mother's voice saying these words. It's important to stay humble and grateful and not get too big for your britches, no matter how much success you're fortunate to have. Treat everyone with respect and kindness, regardless of their life situation or yours. I've worked with a few managers who've gotten a little too full of themselves soon after getting promoted from sales rep to manager, and they forgot how difficult the job is. They began to talk down to reps and speak negatively to senior management about how the reps were performing. I've always felt that I worked for the people I managed, not vice versa. My job as a manager is to provide anything I can to help a rep do their job.

## "If you are patient in one moment of anger, you will escape a hundred days of sorrow." ~ Chinese Proverb

I have this written on a card on my desk and look at it daily.

It took me a few years to embrace this message, and I've failed many times to keep my cool, which has cost me dearly in some situations. It's hard to stay calm when you're angry. It's an ongoing struggle, but when I stay patient instead of becoming outwardly angry, most times, things get better because I stay calm.

There have been times as a rep when a buyer or doctor uses the phrase "You said," and they go on to say something that is absolutely and categorically not what I said. They may quote an incorrect price or policy, and it's very challenging to stay calm and not escalate the misunderstanding. I've learned to use the following statement, "I apologize if there's a misunderstanding on your part regarding this. What I said was ..."

This also reminds me how important it is to get as much in writing as possible in a follow-up message after a meeting about any pricing or policies. I've often re-sent an email confirming what we'd discussed, which has been a great way to ward off a "you said" misunderstanding.

**"Adversity doesn't build character; adversity reveals character." ~ James Allen Lane**

I greatly respect the people I've worked for who provided quality leadership when problems arose. When I worked at Timberland, there were massive inventory shortfalls. The brand had been around for fifty years as a relatively small family business of around fifty million dollars. Suddenly, the brand exploded. Every woman in America wanted the Timberland yellow boot, as did the folks in the inner city. The order rates were hundreds of millions of dollars; however, the factories could only make a fraction of the orders.

The manager I worked for, Ken Snyder, was a Cornell grad and an experienced footwear executive. Everyone was banging on his desk for their shipments: store owners, department store presidents, and every rep and manager, including me. No one gets paid on orders; we make money on shipments. Ken had a big ocean liner to steer, and he did so while never losing his cool. He communicated what would be on hand and set allocations, which no one was happy about, but we were all informed. During these very stressful times, Ken's high character came through. I've thought of him often when things weren't going well, and I've challenged myself to do the right thing and be of high character.

**"When it comes time to perform, everything leaves you except your practice." ~ Anonymous**

This might sound a bit unbelievable, but I hear this mantra in my mind just about every day. I have no idea when I first heard it—probably from a coach I played for. It's stayed with me well beyond its application for playing sports.

My professional life seems to have been all about preparing for something—target lists, calls and presentations, and all we do as reps. The longer I work, the more I prepare. Experience and longevity are factors because the longer I've been working, the more I know what I need to do to succeed. I gain confidence as I practice. Whenever I've ever gone into a sales call or spoken in front of a group and thought I could just wing it, it hasn't gone well. Those failures motivate me to prepare. I must admit that there have also been times when I've frozen and have had to proceed on what I call "automatic pilot," which has saved me. I know that my preparation kicked in during those few moments of being stuck or frozen. The fear of having those scary few minutes when I've gone blank keeps me practicing.

**"I am a great believer in luck, and I find that the harder I work, the more I have of it."**
**~ Thomas Jefferson**

There are many hard days when absolutely nothing happens. There are no emails or calls; it's just dead. Somehow, in some way, I try to make something happen. I try to take some action. I reach out to a new target or an old one I haven't contacted in a while or an existing account to check in or make an unannounced stop to see them. I create a goal for the next hour. Nothing happens by itself, and most times, when I go the extra mile, something good comes from it. Good luck is the result of doing something.

**"It's not the strongest species that survive, nor the most intelligent, but the most responsive to change."**
**~ Charles Darwin**

The survival of the fittest. I've experienced the truth of the above quote first-hand several times. Converse was a major player in athletic footwear, particularly basketball. However, as people started running and women entered the athletic footwear market, Converse didn't adapt to address those consumers. Start-ups like Nike, Reebok, Under Amour, LA Gear, and Skechers saw that the landscape was changing, and they responded to the market's needs and experienced growth and success. Timberland and New Balance are examples of companies that had been small, both less than 50 million dollar enterprises, that grew to billion-dollar global brands by changing and growing as the athletic footwear business grew.

**"We regret the things we don't do more than the things we do." ~ Mark Twain**

I think about this statement in my professional and personal life. On the business side, there have been times when I didn't pursue a customer or held back a more aggressive plan. I remember calling on Footlocker, and while I built a strong working relationship with the basketball buyers and staff, I didn't work very hard at expanding my relationships with the buyers in other categories, particularly women's shoes. I was often at the same events with all the buyers but didn't get to know them or try to build a relationship with them.

I regretted not working my way up the organization when working with some other accounts. I sometimes enjoyed my relationships with the buyers but didn't like the general merchandise manager or the other senior managers. This came back to hurt me if the buyer moved on or the buyer didn't have the clout to pull the trigger on the programs or products I presented. Sometimes when I didn't feel comfortable around certain people, I didn't push through that uneasy feeling to get the job done. These days I work on saying yes to as many proposals and opportunities that come my way so I don't sit on the sidelines.

## FOR FURTHER THOUGHT:

What other favorite quotes inspire you?

# AFTERWORD

I'm working full time as I'm writing this book. I get up early each morning and spend about an hour writing. Then I start my job. Yesterday, I followed up on leads from a VA in New Mexico, two medical products stores in North Carolina and one in Florida, a podiatrist in Indiana, a physical therapist in North Carolina, a hospital in Ohio, and a chiropractor in Pennsylvania. I also spoke with current New York, New Jersey, and Oregon customers. I wrote fifteen emails and had an emergency arise at 4:00 p.m. regarding a top account that required coordinating a team call with customer service and shipping.

The day started at 8:15 a.m. and, after inhaling a quick dinner, ended at 8:00 p.m. I get the same adrenaline rush of calling into leads and juggling the demands of the day as I did when I could hear bouncing basketballs when I walked into a gym to see a recruit play. People ask me from time to time if I'm retired. I guess at a certain age, that comes up. My answer is always that I have no desire to retire. I enjoy being busy and working.

I look forward to the challenges and variety of the job, traveling to all parts of the country, learning new products and programs, and meeting new people. These things keep me recharged and motivated. When I finish each day and close my office door, I ask myself, *What were my wins today?*

# APPENDIX: KEY TIPS AT A GLANCE

Here are some key points to remember from this book:

- Qualities needed for a sales professional: Are you coachable, committed, inspiring, and inspired? Are you a leader? Are you hungry? If you didn't show up today, would you be missed?
- The key objective of a cold call is to secure an appointment. You must have positive energy and be able to engage the gatekeeper.
- While it can be challenging and intimidating to sell against formative competition, every company has unique features and strengths. It's in a buyer's best interest to offer their customers an assortment of products, not only the most popular.
- A request for a discount can be countered by offering company resources that can be more mutually beneficial, such as advertising and marketing support, incentives for sell-through, and product exclusives.
- Studying, preparing, following up, and being consistent builds credibility with the buyer.

- You never have more leverage with an account than before you accept an order. It's as important to walk away from some accounts as it is to start with some. Trust your gut and work with accounts that will present the brand and products in the manner you want.
- Present prewritten orders to assist buyers and provide a blueprint of the type of order you suggest.
- We all have periods of slumps when we aren't motivated. Sales is a lonely profession. Find ways that help you overcome down times. Create personal goals with rewards, take breaks, and help others.
- Consider some form of positive visualization to practice seeing yourself being successful.
- Learn how to travel efficiently and effectively. Establish routines that work for you. Always be early.
- Find mentors and friends and lean on them for advice and support.

# ABOUT THE AUTHOR

Stu Wittner has been a sales professional for forty years since leaving the world of basketball as the country's youngest head college basketball coach at Pace University. His basketball career framed much of his success in sales with so many parallels between the two games. Stu has continued to coach in several youth programs, and he was the head coach of the USA National Men's Team that won the gold medal at the Maccabi Pan Am Games. Stu and his wife, Helene, live in Morristown, New Jersey, close to their children and grandsons.

Printed in the USA
CPSIA information can be obtained
at www.ICGtesting.com
JSHW010220200124
55349JS00013B/289